Teaching with Feeling

Teaching

Compassion and Self-Awareness

with Feeling

in the Classroom Today

Dr. Herbert M. Greenberg

PEGASUS

A Division of the Bobbs-Merrill, Co., Inc., Publishers
Indianapolis

The Bobbs-Merrill Company, Inc.
4300 West 62nd Street
Indianapolis, Indiana 46206

Library of Congress Catalog Card Number: 69-13393
Published by arrangement with The Macmillan Company

ISBN 0-672-63601-8 (pbk)
First Pegasus edition 1970
Fifth printing—1975

To my children, Laurie and Randy,

the hope of the future

Contents

Foreword

DR. GREENBERG HERE OFFERS A BOOK THAT WILL BE OF great value to teachers and, indirectly, to pupils and parents. He leads us into a dimension of teaching that is more often ignored than explored—the subjective dimension, consisting of the private thoughts and feelings teachers have about pupils, supervisors, colleagues, and parents, and the feelings they have about themselves. These feelings, whether obliquely expressed or kept under cover like a guilty secret, influence every phase of a teacher's relationships with pupils and associates. A policy of ignoring "what moves and stirs the teacher in the long run results in a loss to the child."

Dr. Greenberg's exploration of teachers' feelings and needs is sensitive, earthy, and profound. He warmly acknowledges the contribution made to this book by teachers who were willing, and had the courage, to look at themselves. This document clearly reflects the humanity of these teachers. But it is equally clear that Dr. Greenberg, through his own insight and humanity, has been able to give voice to feelings and strivings that usually are deviously expressed or remain mute and unspoken.

ARTHUR T. JERSILD

Professor
Teachers College
Columbia University

Preface

THIS BOOK OFFERS NO PANACEAS OR EASY SOLUTIONS. IT IS merely an attempt to open up for public consideration a significant area of the teacher's life—his inner world, his feelings, his emotional being.

This book is based on the assumption that human feelings comprise the most perplexing and yet most powerful area of human expression and interaction. For this reason alone the relevance of human feelings in the teacher is worthy of discussion and attention. But since feelings are unavoidably complex and personally disturbing, this book offers no simple answers or techniques. It is hoped, however, that this volume will find empathetic response in teachers, teachers-to-be, and parents, as they gaze within themselves and recognize the common humanity of their feelings. This response in itself would be a significant step toward countering those immensely powerful dehumanizing trends that have unfortunately been developing in education, in parenthood, and in other crucial areas of our lives.

The author owes immeasurable gratitude to the many teachers, other educators, and parents who over the years shared their innermost experiences with him. The material in this book is in one sense a kind of documentary account of what they have actually experienced and felt. The many, many persons who contributed to it through their own acts of self-disclosure are the true authors.

11

Though it is impossible to thank each of these numerous contributors individually, certain individuals gave of themselves fully over long periods of time. Flora Coley, Carol Ely, Reba Gillman, Julie Guttman, Barbara Merrill, and Lillian Roemer are teachers and supervisors who have shared much with the author as they involved themselves in self-discovery over many years. Principals Mary Kinsella, Clayton Buck, and Willard Peters, to name but a few, co-operated in this venture by making available to their faculties the opportunity to share their feelings. My wife, Phyllis, has opened up many avenues of human feeling to me through her own unique personal sensitivity and support. Moreover, she offered a considerable amount from her experience as a school social worker.

This book is written for the many teachers and parents whom I hope it will encourage and support in their struggle for self-hood.

H. M. G.

July 28, 1968

Teaching with Feeling

Introduction

WE ARE LOOKING, ON AN OCTOBER DAY, AT A TYPICAL elementary school in this country. It could be located in the suburbs north of Chicago, in Westchester County, or in the San Fernando Valley of Los Angeles. It could be in the inner-city area of such a large metropolitan district as New York City; or in a more sparsely populated farming district in almost any of the fifty states. As we walk down the corridor there is the quiet hum of children at work. Suddenly these mild educational sounds are disrupted by the bursting open of a classroom door. A young teacher rushes out. She is obviously overwrought and bursts into tears as she flees down the hall. This scene is not infrequent. It occurs in thousands of schools each year.

This young teacher is new to teaching. She has just completed four years of college and earned a teacher's certificate. She has had an excellent teacher preparation program with at least thirty-six credit hours in the field of Elementary Education, including fifteen weeks of practice teaching in an actual classroom. She has studied a host of courses in the arts and sciences and an impressive number of courses in an academic concentration outside the field of education. She has studied the psychology of children, how they learn, their characteristics, their needs, their feelings.

Though her preparation was excellent and her current supervision helpful, she feels very ill-prepared to teach

15

children as she flees down the hall. The professional assistance she received suffered from a most serious omission: The emotional life of the teacher was not a subject of study or concern. She's had no study of teacher development, teacher needs, teachers' feelings. She's not had one course in teacher psychology. None were offered. Now, after less than a month of full responsibility in the classroom, she is struggling to cope with her own feelings.

She finds actual teaching radically different from her practice-teaching assignment. She no longer has a master teacher close by to steer her away from trouble, to rescue her when things get out of hand, to relieve her from the lonely pressures of continuous hour-by-hour teaching. She suffers from intense feelings of inadequacy and is deeply concerned about the principal's evaluation of her. She is terrified when he enters her classroom. She frequently compares herself to other teachers in the school and often feels vastly inferior. She feels almost pure horror as she looks forward to next week's PTA open house, at which she expects to be inundated by as many as thirty sets of parents. In many schools these parents will be highly educated, and very interested in their children's school achievements. In other schools, parents may be openly hostile. Our teacher anticipates that some of these parents will have doubts about her ability to successfully teach their children and prepare them for eventual admission into college.

She is also struggling with her feelings about children. Most of them behave rather well, but she has already developed a strong dislike for several of them. A few of the boys are remarkably skilled at making her look ridiculous with their smirking and muttering. Each time her back is turned, she anticipates another flagrant incident, accompanied by giggling and other disrespectful noises. She finds herself continually stifling her natural emotional reactions and struggling to hold back growing feelings of irritation or annoyance. By midday they flare out, and the accumulated anger may be directed toward an innocent child. She then feels guilt and shame, which add to her emotional burden. To make matters worse, she feels uneasy and a little guilty about those children she likes, and therefore even her warm, accepting feelings seem soured.

This teacher is struggling with her feelings—very real, very strong feelings. She even has doubts whether teaching is the profession for her. These fears she also keeps mainly to herself. Occasionally she reveals them to a friend, but her profession, the field of education, ignores them. Probably this new teacher will survive her first year. Her second will be easier as she learns to adjust on her own, but perhaps some of her children will have a troubled and unsuccessful year. Could some of this turmoil and failure have been avoided? Can inexperienced teachers be given direct assistance in coping with their feelings?

The scene now shifts to the teachers' room in another school. The time is about noon. Several teachers are taking a break while their children are eating or in special classes. They are obviously attempting to relax, to let off some of the steam that has accumulated after several hours of uninterrupted teaching. One teacher appears weary and tired, another tense and nervous, another worried and concerned. Dialogue varies:

"I just can't stand that Robbins boy."

"Millie is having one of her days, and it's driving me crazy."

"I wonder what I can make for supper tonight."

"Today is just one of those days."

"Oh, you poor thing, I had him last year, and he is impossible."

One teacher sits quietly in the corner. Today brought a visit by a supervisor, crucial to tenure evaluation. Another teacher broods secretly about her own child, sick at home, left with a baby-sitter while she has gone to work in school. One of the younger teachers brims with enthusiasm over a child. An experienced teacher sounds almost smug as she reports on her morning.

It seems that many of the teachers, in the relative privacy of the teachers' room, are able to let their hair down and reveal something of their inner selves. Out pour the pressures of the day, their home and personal problems, their joys and their fears. Here, too, jealousy is exposed, competition for the principal's approval is expressed, and real feelings about coworkers are revealed. For some their inner life is laid bare; for others only part is exposed. Some gain reassurance about themselves; others leave with heightened anxiety. Whether it is a newly acquired reassurance or an aroused anxiety, these feelings affect her performance in the classroom. They affect the teacher's patience in dealing with children, the teacher's ability to discipline children successfully, and especially the teacher's ability to sustain exciting, interesting learning for children. Here again is lost opportunity. Often these feelings are considered irrelevant; usually they are ignored. At best the teacher is expected to "control" them, which usually means to mask, cover up, and deny what the teacher deeply feels. Shouldn't such feelings be recognized rather than ignored, dealt with directly rather than masked, considered natural rather than shameful or a sign of weakness?

Now we shift to a school in the inner city of a large metropolitan area. This could be in Oakland, Chicago, Philadelphia, Rochester, Boston, or any other urban school district. Most of the children are Negro or Puerto Rican. Their background is the slum. Some are dirty and tattered, others clean, but scared. Some are highly sensitive to criticism, others have failed for years and apparently no longer care. Fights frequently break out, accompanied by abusive, obscene language. These children talk of a world radically different from modern middle-class suburbia: a world of sex, of violence, of racial hate; of hunger, drugs, prostitution; of welfare, poverty, hopelessness.

Entering this scene most typically is a middle-class teacher. She has been brought up in a middle-class neighborhood or suburb and educated in a middle-class college. This person has carefully and successfully avoided contacts with people in the slums and has had little positive experience with minority groups. Thus she has been reasonably well protected from the sordidness, the violence, the horror of poverty. In addition, this teacher is most typically white; whereas the children she teaches are most typically Negro, Puerto Rican, or Mexican-American.

The teacher's contact with this widely different culture almost always results in shock—sheer emotional shock: feelings of horror and disgust, intense fear, and even hatred. Feelings of racial prejudice, only dimly recognized in the past, frequently emerge, accompanied by shame, guilt, and defensiveness. Pity and sympathy vacillate with fright and anger. These feelings are aroused by a child picking his nose, another masturbating, a five-year-old letting loose with a blast of four-letter words, girls pulling hair and screaming obscenities, children telling openly and frankly of sexual behavior—relating stories that arouse disgust mixed with fascination, shame mixed with curiosity.

A most typical human response to such a barrage of intense emotional experience is sheer numbness—emotional withdrawal, apathy, hopelessness. And here in the slums, where education is the sole hope for so many, here it is that the teacher's emotions are so devoid of hope. To cope with feelings that are so new, so raw, so intense, the teacher may give up all feeling and withdraw emotionally. A most frequent criticism of teachers in the slums is that they no longer care—no longer provide hope and inspiration; no longer burst with the excitement of learning.

Here again the educational establishment has been slow to admit the importance of the teachers' feelings, to face squarely the emotional impact of cultural shock and the kinds of adjustments middle-class teachers must make to the slum child. The professional concern over poverty education has focused instead on the mechanical and curricular aspects of teaching. The building, the equipment, the materials, the textbooks, are all vital to teaching. What is most vital, however, is an alive and feeling teacher; one who cares, hopes, and inspires. How can teachers in the slums cope with their feelings and still sustain excitement and hope? Can ways be found to help the middle-class teacher deal with the emotional shock of slum life and racism?

These examples from typical educational settings illustrate the obvious—that teachers do indeed have feelings. Inevitably and quite naturally, teachers react with the full range of human, emotional response: Teachers feel alive, excited, enthusiastic, or depressed, apathetic, miserable. They may feel inadequate, inferior, confused, uncertain, even helpless. They can and do feel irritated, annoyed, angry, jealous. They also feel loving, delighted, affectionate, and even sexually stimulated. They can feel terrified or ridiculous, ashamed or humiliated. They can dislike, they can hate. Teaching can be, and is, pleasureable and joyous, frustrating and hell. Teachers are human beings.

The theme of this book is that within the teacher's emotional life are the forces that most powerfully affect the entire teaching process. The human, emotional qualities of the teacher are the very heart of teaching. No matter how much emphasis is placed on such other qualities in teaching as educational technique, technology, equipment, or buildings, *the humanity of the teacher is the vital ingredient if children are to learn.* Exploration of the full range and depth of the feelings of teachers enhances our understanding of this basic ingredient. Moreover, it provides us with a tool that sheds considerable light on some of the crucial school problems that plague educators and parents alike.

In this book a number of these problems will be discussed. They include numerous learning and behavior problems of children, struggles of teachers learning to live with themselves and with others, concerns of parents which arise out of their children's school problems, and the responsibilities of supervisors, college professors, and others who direct the training and development of teachers.

Problems of children in the classroom are of concern not only to teachers but of course to the children themselves and their parents. In this book we will look at problems of child success and failure, the disruptive behavior of children in the classroom, so-called personality conflicts between children and teacher, and discipline problems. In addition there will be special focus on some of the sources in the teacher of the gross educational failures in slum schools.

When teachers discuss their own problems in teaching, many of their concerns are not directly aroused by children but rather by persons outside the classroom walls. These feelings are created primarily by the home and personal life of the teacher, by supervisors, principals, and other teachers, and by the teacher's efforts to relate to the parents of the children in her classroom. The feelings aroused by these relationships will be discussed in this book. These feelings will be viewed openly and realistically in an effort to show how their impact on the teacher's performance in the classroom can be minimized.

Inexperienced teachers have special problems of their own. Thousands of new teachers enter our schools each year. They engage, as in any profession, in a long and at times agonizing process as they gain competence and confidence. During college training, the teacher-to-be also faces many experiences fraught with emotional struggle. In this book the long period of learning and practice will be viewed in terms of those normal and natural emotional adjustments that human beings make in dealing with new and intense experiences. This point of view will inevitably have implications for the selection of teachers, their preparation, and their supervision on the job.

Parents have a host of problems associated with schools, which are highly charged with the most personal and deeply felt feelings. Children are a most intimate extension of the parent's own self. As such they strongly reflect the parents' feelings of satisfaction and adequacy. Many of the feelings of parents, moreover, bear a strong resemblance to the feelings of teachers. Parents and teachers suffer some of the same tortures, agonies, and joys, just as they share responsibility for the learning, social development, and discipline of children. Moreover, both parents and teachers soon discover that their own self-esteem is closely tied to the child's performance in school. Because of this, parents and teachers often feel uncomfortable with each other. They may even be fearful of each other, and attempt to blame or impress one another. In this book parents will be able to recognize many of their own feelings as they read about how teachers really feel.

The feelings and problems analyzed in this book have been assembled from a great many discussions held by the author with teachers, other educators, and parents. These discussions gave teachers and parents an opportunity to share the feelings and concerns they had in working with and living with children. With teachers, these discussions took place over a period of many years in faculty meetings, special workshops, supervisory sessions, in-service courses, graduate seminars, college courses, educational conferences, and personal consultations. At times these sessions were offered to educational administrators, school psychologists, guidance counselors, and other school personnel. Administrators and other educators have feelings too, and these emotions are extremely important in understanding their relationships with teachers and children. Discussions with parents took place primarily in group discussion sessions sponsored in a variety of parent education programs developed and administered by the author in suburbs, metropolitan areas, and inner-city poverty projects. Group discussions with parents provide many insights into the feelings of parents.

In discussing teachers' feelings in each of the problem areas, certain significant questions will be asked: What kinds of child behavior arouse feelings in teachers? What kinds of feelings are aroused, and what are the sources of these feelings in the teacher's own background and personality? What are some of the typical ways teachers cope with their feelings? How do these different means of adjustment to feelings affect children, parents, and others? And perhaps the most significant question of this book, how can teachers deal with their feelings in ways that are not harmful to themselves, to children, and to parents?

1

Teacher or Myth?

EACH TEACHER DAILY FACES THE REALITY OF HIS OWN teaching behavior. He continually experiences real, honest feelings. He continuously acts, behaves, and reacts in the classroom. In addition to this reality, however wonderful or painful it may be, most teachers also carry within themselves another reality that can be a nagging, painful burden. This inner reality is composed of myths—overidealized notions about what a teacher should be like, how a teacher should behave, what a teacher should be feeling or not feeling. These myths develop and grow from many sources—from college courses, education professors, observing master teachers, supervisors, books about education, parents, and other teachers. Like many growths, these myths become weedy, if not cancerous. They may bind or strangle the teacher in a rigid web of painful self-evaluation. They often bear little resemblance to the teacher's daily reality. But they persist, they pervade the teacher's very being. They provide the teacher with a set of overidealized goals. They secretly whisper to the teacher a barrage of shoulds and should-nots. These are incessant,

24

thorough, and powerful. They add immeasurably to the burden of teaching.

The discrepancy between the teacher's actual feelings and these persistent myths burden the teacher with uneasiness and guilt: "I am not being what I should be," "I am feeling what I should not be feeling," "What if someone (the principal, parent, other teachers) finds out what I am really like?"

The teacher must then cope not only with the reality of teaching, which may be difficult enough, but also with these inner voices of superidealism and guilt.

These myths are true fantasies. No one behaves consistently in an ideal fashion. These myths are dangerous. They sap the teacher's inner strengths by weakening his self-confidence and denying the uniqueness of each teacher as a separate, special human being.

What are these myths? First, the *Myth of Calmness.* Teachers are expected to behave calmly and coolly at all times. They must cope with all situations quietly and confidently. They must face the child picking his nose, the child crying, the temper tantrum, the obscene language, all with an attitude of sureness and ease. No matter how excited or tired, the teacher is expected to be emotionally stable, emotionally consistent. This myth insists that the teacher not display any of her real feeling or mood. No matter how joyous or angry, these feelings, too, must be hidden, disguised, "controlled." Calmness and serenity, keeping "one's cool," are essential to this fantasy. It is, of course, suprahuman and therefore inhuman to expect teachers to never feel anger or shakiness, joy or helplessness. Yet this myth persists, and many a teacher is plagued by it whenever the calmness and confidence are lost and replaced by more typically human and natural feelings.

Related to this is the *Myth of Moderation*, to which our

society persistently clings. In spite of almost continual wars, assassination of our national leaders, violence in our cities, conflict between management and labor, and a host of examples all around us of extreme and radical behavior, we persist in believing that the normal human life is one of moderation. We elect presidents who are "middle-of-the-roaders," we look on extreme feelings as "immature." Our Anglo-Saxon, Victorian tradition still plagues us with the British ideal (but not reality) of sophistication, reasonableness, and a calm attitude toward life. We associate extreme expression of feelings with the hot-blooded Mediterranean countries or with the "childlike" behavior of the American Negro. They are frowned upon, viewed as inferior, considered socially "out" and psychologically immature. The result is an ideal that smacks of numbness, blah, and nothingness. The purveyors of this myth insist that the mentally "healthy" person has no problems that can't be dealt with mildly, has few conflicts, and rarely experiences extreme or strong feelings. Almost all feelings are rejected by these myths, and especially feelings that overcome us with their intensity, their depth, their pain.

There is growing awareness that these myths are ridiculous, unrealistic. It is becoming more fashionable to feel life fully in the theater, in art, in movies—but not yet in the classroom, or in life itself.

Another persistent myth unfortunately promulgated by teacher training institutions is the one that says *children's feelings are more important than teacher's feelings.* Children's feelings are frequently thought to be influenced by the teacher, the learning process, and by other children. This myth ignores the other direction of influence; child behavior has a tremendous influence on the feeling of the teacher. We must not consider solely the effect that the teacher has on the child, but must consider also the crucial and powerful effect that most children have on the feelings of teachers.

This myth is fostered by courses in child psychology that completely ignore the psychology of the teacher. Any parent or teacher or other person who has lived or worked with children has been influenced, sometimes with joy, other times with misery, by the behavior of children.

A parent or teacher who denies his own feelings is wrapped in stress and struggle. One result of this struggle is that spontaneity and warmth are drowned in resentment and conflict. Children's feelings can be considered sincerely and reasonably only to the extent that the teacher considers honestly and realistically his own feelings. It is difficult, if not impossible, to deny pressing needs of one's own, while attempting to meet the needs of others. A teacher who expresses his own feelings, moreover, sets a climate in which children's feelings are also acceptable and understood.

The *"I Love All Children" Myth* is another fantasy that blatantly disregards the humanity of the teacher. This myth incorporates the fallacy of liking all children the same, of having no dislikes for specific children or specific behavior in children. This also denies the depth and complexity of love in the teaching relationship. The concept of love, complex as it is, mobilizes some of the most disturbing confusions for human beings. As love is fully realized, it inevitably includes a variety of other feelings, including anger if not hate, loss and separation, with accompanying anxiety and a variety of fears, rejections, and hurts. Many teachers do recognize that they feel love in relationships with children. However, to be able to love all children is a basic denial of one's special uniqueness and of the true complexity of love. To feel joy and excitement in the freshness and newness of the young as they reach out to experience their world is a special privilege available to the teacher. To feel love for all children in the classroom is blatantly unrealistic.

Related to this unrealistic view of the teacher is the *"I Treat All Children Alike"* or *"Consistency" Myth.* To treat all children alike at the very least denies special feelings for individual children. In addition this myth rejects normal favoritism, inevitable dislike, and a host of special feelings which teachers feel for each child in the classroom. Children are handled individually and differently by teachers. They are not all treated the same each hour, day, or week. Each child arouses a special and unique encounter with each teacher because of his uniqueness. If looked at crossly by the teacher one child bursts into tears, while another can be punished, yelled, and screamed at without apparent upset. What is successful at nine in the morning may not work at all at three in the afternoon. One child requires delicate handling, another stern firmness; one requires detachment, another closeness; one arouses in the teacher a special warmth, another provokes anger, disgust, or rejection. To survive a normal teaching day, teachers must choose with great care which behavior to deal with and which to let go by. If teachers handled all situations in the same way, almost the entire teaching day would be composed of nothing but "nos," "stops," and "don'ts."

The *Permissive Myth* is another fallacy held dear by some teachers. The notion here is that permitting children behavior which is really unacceptable to adults is somehow good and healthy for them. Teachers and parents are led to believe that no matter what annoyance or other negative reaction is aroused by the child's behavior, that behavior should nevertheless be permitted. This is a misguided interpretation of the accepting role of the psychotherapist, who is also concerned with what is good and health-giving for his client. Psychologists, however, do not live with their client six or eight or twenty-four hours per day as teachers and parents do. If they did, their accepting behavior would be badly shattered. In fact, this accept- ance is sometimes shaken even in a single one-hour ses- sion.

Many teachers can be observed struggling to com- fortably permit and accept a variety of child behaviors which actually arouse irritation, anger, and negative re- sponse. This myth dies hard, but actually was never really practiced by most teachers. Saying "Johnny, isn't that nice" as he spreads blue paint over his arms is simply a down- right lie for most adults. The child easily senses the true emotional response of the teacher. Attempting to permit what we emotionally reject makes this myth a farce.

A related myth is the *"Children Need to be Protected from the Teacher's Feelings" Myth*. Somehow children are seen as so delicate and weak that they should be smothered only in the most positive, sweetest, and gentlest of feelings. Teachers who believe this myth often try to be especially nice and overly sweet to children. "It would be nice if you considered the other children, Johnny," "every- thing is wonderful," or "you're doing *so* well." There is an overabundance of praise, called for or not. Children are flooded with slightly artificial, not tremendously sincere positive expressions. Children are seen as having little inner strengths, no resiliency, meager self-esteem. They must, according to this myth, be continuously bathed in a "nice," praiseworthy, smooth, pleasant atmosphere. This climate must be devoid of tension, stress, and conflict; all of which would apparently cause these delicate creatures to fall apart. The learning potential of failure, disappoint- ment, and frustration are considered so horrible as to be avoided at all costs. In a world full of struggle and conflict, this view of the child's learning condition is ludicrous. Before the child even enters school, he has faced consider- able stress, conflict, and anger within the typical family situation. Disagreements between parents, angry discipline, and sibling jealousy are normal experiences for all children. And these experiences are loaded with strong feeling. By the time the child starts kindergarten, he has had extensive preparation in learning to deal with a variety of the feelings experienced by adults. Most of them survive this family emotional barrage fairly well—all make some kind of adjustment and learn somehow to live with the feelings of adults.

To attempt to perpetuate this fantasy requires, moreover, that the teacher deny the meaning of human life and experience—the excitement, tension, struggling, and uncertainty of being a person, of growing up, of relating to others. As Sartre says "Hell is other people," and the child has already learned before his formal education begins that he must learn to live with this kind of existence.

A continuous, positive, warm, affectionate adult relationship is impossible to maintain. Continuous praise is not sincere, it's not real, and kids know it. The teacher who tries to be positive, but does not really feel positive, is attempting a fraud which rarely comes off.

This myth can only persist in conjunction with an equally fantastic fallacy: The *"I Can Hide My True Feelings from Children" Myth.* This "they don't really know how I feel" belief may be a reassuring one to the teacher who is struggling to hide and deny what he truly feels. Children or other outsiders, however, are rarely fooled by the efforts of teachers (or parents) to hide the emotions that are bursting underneath. Even when such feelings have not reached explosive proportions, they are revealed in very subtle ways. The teacher's spontaneity is one major loss—excitement, interest, and enthusiasm are blunted if not completely obliterated. Some teachers feel more tense, others tire easily or are overcome by emotional if not physical exhaustion. Trying to hide or disguise feelings requires great effort. Much energy is expended, and emotional exhaustion is typical at the end of such a teaching day.

Most teachers realize that their feelings are revealed, sometimes directly, more often indirectly. "They seep through," "children are very sensitive to feelings," a facial expression, a tone of voice. One teacher reported the verbal frauds she engages in when angry. When the kids get out of hand, she coolly calls out: "I beg your pardon." The kids translate this: "For Christ's sake, shut up." Or, when a child leaves the room without permission, she again states with apparent calm, "I beg your pardon." The class translates this as: "Get the hell back in the room."

But many teachers know that children appreciate being treated openly and honestly. Children are then encouraged to deal more honestly with their own feelings and thereby gain better control of them.

The *"I Have No Favorites" Myth* dies hard for some teachers who insist that they feel the same toward all children and treat them all the same way. To deny favoring one child over another is to deny having any particular interest as a person. Each teacher does have unique interests and responds to children who share these interests. They favor those children with more time, attention, energy, effort, and excitement. Each teacher has certain personality traits they favor. Children who possess these traits are reacted to with more spontaneous affection. The kind of person the teacher normally likes, whether an adult or child, receives a "favoring" of one sort or another from teachers. Some teachers favor boys over girls, or girls over boys. Trying to deny one's favoring feelings inevitably gets one into the "I can hide my feelings" game, with all the consequences of self-deception and lack of sincerity.

Another myth that has special relevance in our times of

racial tension and strife is the *"I Have No Prejudices"* *Myth*. This myth has lost some of its credibility with the advent of current racial rioting, but it is still considered the ideal attitude for teachers to assume. The fact is, prejudices exist in all of us. They are based on ethnic, national, religious, and the socioeconomic groups with which we identify. As the laws on discrimination put it, prejudice exists on the basis of "color, creed, religion," even "sex and age."

We have prejudices or prejudgments about *all* people, not just those groups listed in the laws. We prejudge men, women, college students, fraternity members, teachers, principals, Jews, Catholics, Poles, and Irishmen; businessmen and baseball players, blacks and whites. We prejudge individuals solely on the basis of their membership in a group. As we get to know people individually, these prejudices are often discarded. But when we first meet people, or when we merely hear or read about them, we prejudge on the basis of preconceived projections.

The prejudgments may be mild or strong, conscious or unconscious. They almost always carry feelings of inferiority and superiority—one group feels inferior to another; the other in turn feels superior. The Kerner report on civil disorders (The Riot Commission) used the phrase "White Racism" to describe white-black superiority/inferiority status in our society. We also have religions, nationalities, occupations, country clubs, neighborhoods, etc., which are superior groups, and in turn, religious, national, etc., groups which are inferior. If you were brought up in American society as a white, it is inevitable that you have prejudices about blacks. If you are an American Negro, it is inevitable that you have prejudices about whites. These prejudices are not easy for many teachers to admit. It used to be quite fashionable for a white teacher when asked how many Negro children were in her class to answer, self-righteously, "I don't know, I'll have to count tomorrow." This attitude toward racial differences is rapidly disappearing, as is the old superficial attempts at "once a year brotherhood," and the comfort of "everything is going well in the ghetto."

Prejudices are normal, inevitable, and in fact quite necessary in helping people know how to interact with a human being before they get to know him personally. Teachers have feelings about the little Jewish boy, the Irish child, the Negro, the "poor" kid, the son of the doctor, etc., which are based on prejudgments. Trouble occurs when the child behaves in a way that lends support to the teacher's (and society's) stereotype about the group to which the child belongs. If the Jewish boy talks loud and behaves aggressively, or the Negro child acts lazy but has a good sense of rhythm, then the teacher finds support for society's stereotype.

The danger lies in attributing loud, aggressive, or lazy behavior to the group the child is a member of, and thereby consciously or unconsciously denying or being unable to see any other traits the child possesses. All children can be loud, aggressive, and lazy. The questions to be asked are: Why is this child? What are his strengths? The teacher who responds solely in terms of feelings of prejudice never gets to raise these other questions. The teacher's emotional support of a stereotype inevitably gets in the way.

This danger is compounded because stereotypes have a self-fulfilling nature. The Jewish boy who is rejected by the teacher because he's aggressive feels hurt and anger; he probably will deal with his hurt and anger by acting more aggressive and louder. The teacher will find support for her prejudices. The Negro child who is rejected by the teacher because he is "lazy" feels hurt and a loss of pride. This child may handle his feelings by withdrawing from the teacher, adding more fuel to the teacher's stereotype of Negro "lack of interest in school" and "laziness."

The real issue for teachers, as for all of us, is not whether we do or do not possess prejudices, but whether we can honestly recognize them in ourselves. Only by admitting and facing our inevitable prejudices can we hope to deal with them effectively, to make up for them, compensate for them, or otherwise undo any damage caused by them. Human beings inevitably hurt others; in fact we sometimes deeply hurt the persons we love the most. To face this honestly is the first necessary step for moving on to more positive relationships between persons and groups.

Another myth held at times by teachers can badly shake up their emotions. This is the *"I Have to Know All the Answers" Myth,* sometimes read as the "teachers should make no mistakes" belief, or the more painful "I have to be perfect" fantasy.

Many teachers recognize that this myth gets them "into a box" quite frequently. With new curricula sprouting up almost constantly, teachers find it difficult to keep up with all the new concepts, methods, ideas, and content. Children are learning so much today, and at an earlier age than in past years, that teachers have to keep stepping just to keep up.

Some children delight in discovering the teacher who is particularly insecure about his lack of knowledge or a new teacher or someone teaching a subject for the first time. If a teacher derives his feelings of competence and adequacy from knowing all the answers, he's in for trouble. Sooner or later someone will catch him with his answers down. A French teacher reported how certain kids seem deliberately out to get her—"Have you ever lived in France?" Luckily, she had. "Then what's the French word for ————?" and he blurted out some technical term she didn't even know in English. "Teachers don't have to know all the answers. Your parents, all adults, make mistakes— it's not so bad not to be perfect," or simply, "Look it up in the dictionary or the encyclopedia or the library," which then becomes a lesson for the child in learning to use other sources than the teacher—all these replies are valid.

This myth can be patched up, bandaged, covered with hesitation and embarrassment. It can also be discarded for the more human point of view. Increasingly teachers are becoming more able to do just that and accept their own normal inadequacies. Catching adults making mistakes can be fun for children. What a comfort when Mommy spills milk at the dinner table! And to catch a teacher in a spelling or arithmetic mistake can be pure joy! Children learn to accept their own mistakes when teachers and parents are able to admit their imperfections. There is also less need to lie about one's failures, to blame someone else for one's mistakes, or to attack the questioner who asks the unknown question.

Two additional myths create emotional problems for teachers who subscribe to them. First, there is the *"Learning Can Take Place Without Confusion and Uncertainty"* *Myth*. Learning is visualized by teachers who hold dearly to this myth as the acquisition (mainly through memorization) of clear, distinct, definite ideas or concepts. The child is seen as moving from one point of sureness and clarity to another. The fallacy here is that new learning cannot be taken from the teacher and given to the student all wrapped up neatly and clearly. The student must achieve his own understanding, and, to achieve understanding, he must begin with lack of understanding. This starts with a question, a doubt, a feeling of confusion and uncertainty. In order to learn something new, it's absolutely essential that one start from this point.

The emotional problem here is that many adults and some children cannot tolerate uncertainty. They are not comfortable with confusion. They feel a sense of inadequacy, a growing anxiety, which must be driven away. Such teachers, sensing the feeling of uncertainty or confusion in themselves or in children, rapidly offer answers, solutions, ways of looking at things. The child in turn must then acquire and accept the teacher's certainty whether it makes sense to him or not. John Holt, in *How Children Fail,* points out the numerous strategies children adopt, not to learn, but to please the teacher who desperately wants the certainty and clarity of an answer. Learning in the classroom requires then that teachers possess ability to live comfortably with confusion and uncertainty. They must not hold onto this myth by forcing children to take refuge in memorization.

The second related myth refers to the teacher and the child's process of growth and change. Many teachers believe that, if not here, then somewhere out there is a normal process of growth, which is smooth, pleasant, and devoid of struggle and conflict. This is the myth that the *"Mature" Teacher or Child Should Cope with Life Without Stress, Anxiety, and Conflict.* Change and growth in oneself and others should be a relatively comfortable, smooth process with few hang-ups and no severe feelings.

None of us knows anyone who has coped with life this way, except for a few liars and those we do not know well enough to discover what their inner hells are truly like. Nevertheless, the myth persists. Life should be devoid of fear, frustration, failure; we can somehow avoid agony, misery, and hurt. The "well-adjusted" person has minimum conflicts, hates, and hang-ups. The "mature" adult or child has no nightmares, daydreams, escape needs. Of course, this is pure baloney. It is based on the outmoded homeostasis theory of the human body, which visualized persons as normally existing in a comfortable, easy state only occasionally disrupted by some drive or need, usually nasty or negative. This "abnormal" condition is eliminated as soon as this disrupting need is met or realized, and the human body then returns to its "normal" state of quietude and rest.

A more recent point of view reverses completely what is "normal" and what is "abnormal." The normal condition is not of rest and comfort, but of activity, action, and struggle. Anxiety, stress, and tension are required to sustain this activity, and a host of extreme emotions inevitably accompany our struggles. Rest, quiet, inactivity, and passivity are for most human beings intolerable. Try to do nothing, absolutely nothing, for any length of time. Boredom, restlessness, and activity will quickly emerge as a powerful replacement for doing nothing. Even our vacations must be filled with activity and action, whether it be reading, physical activity, or even active thinking and feeling.

The teacher who looks at his own growth and coping in terms of this myth finds severe deviations from the so-called "normal" in his every contact with children and with himself. Many teachers recognize that the excitement of anxiety and challenge is the very zest of teaching. When they are involved and struggling, they do indeed feel most alive!

2

Likes and Dislikes

MISS LINDSAY IS A THIRD GRADE TEACHER. SHE IS GOING over the list of names of the twenty-eight children in her class. Instead of grading them on their competence in Social Studies, English, or Arithmetic, she is reacting to each child in terms of her own feelings of like or dislike. Miss Lindsay tries to do this as honestly as she can, and she comes across a number of children on the list whom she can unequivocably admit liking. Mary is cute and feminine; John is bright and alert; Ellen is a real pleaser; Allan is "all boy"; Nancy quietly does excellent work; George is responsive and eager; Sharon is highly musical. Other names on the list arouse clear and instant dislike. Burt is a bully and mean; Bobby disobeys flagrantly; Jane is somewhat of a smug know-it-all; Louis's father is a big shot in the community; Arthur is loud, noisy, and aggressive; Anne clings and whines a great deal; Arnie is awfully untidy.

Other children arouse mixed and varying feelings in Miss Lindsay. She likes some things about them, and dislikes other things. Bill is active and masculine, but sometimes gets out of hand; Tom is quietly nice, but easily gives up when he can't succeed; Laverne is outgoing and vivacious, but tattles on the other children; Jack is brilliant, but bored with most schoolwork. For a few children Miss Lindsay has very little feeling one way or the other. They are blah, indistinct, almost unknown to her, even though she has had several months to get to know them. They just do not stand out at all.

It is impossible for teachers not to have likes and dislikes. It is impossible to feel the same way toward all children. Human beings inevitably react uniquely and specifically to other human beings. Miss Lindsay has had a lifetime to form her own personal likes and dislikes in people. She cannot shed them in class.

Physical appearance and mannerisms can influence our liking and disliking. Another powerful factor is the similarity of the teacher's own interests and hobbies to a child's interests and hobbies. These likes and dislikes are generally idiosyncratic in that they arise solely from the person and personality of each teacher. Miss Lindsay loves music, plays the piano well, and is especially delighted with a child who is highly musical. Mr. Jones likes Gene because his shuffling, awkward physical movements remind Mr. Jones nostalgically of himself as a child. The charming, quiet smile of Janie arouses for Mr. Harvey a pleasurable recall of his own younger sister.

Appearances, manners, gestures, ways of speaking and relating to others, all affect our likes and dislikes. Mrs. Waingate likes precise, careful, cautious, reserved people. The children she teaches who possess these characteristics have a special place for her. Mrs. Arno prefers open, expansive, outgoing, expressive, and emotional people. She warms up easily and spontaneously to children who possess these traits and is less liable to like the cautious, reserved child. She may, in fact, become more easily annoyed or impatient over the child who makes up his mind slowly or responds sluggishly to her efforts.

Some teachers recognize how important their own interests are in liking a child. "The things I like to do, the out of school things—mechanics, reading, hiking, water skiing, bridge, scrabble." The teacher who says, "I love to do creative writing" responds personally to the child who "comes up with an interesting phrase."

Affection for individual children is influenced by many personal factors. Mrs. Martin has spontaneous liking for George. George is a "hellion on wheels," a 100 percent American boy. He always gets into everything, he's a mischief maker, always in trouble, but she loves him. Mrs. Martin has been teaching for years, and this kind of child has always delighted her. "I prefer all boy," she says with great feeling, and she always has.

Mrs. Varalis has a younger brother for whom she has always had especially fond and tender feelings. Her brother is not yet ready to settle down and take life seriously. He's well behaved, but does things only halfway. He has ability but hasn't yet been able to demonstrate it in school. Whenever Mrs. Varalis has a child in class who resembles her younger brother in his inability to "take hold of things," she has special understanding of this child. She easily transfers her feelings of love and sympathy for her brother to any child with similar problems.

Miss Joy teaches mathematics. She likes the order and certainty of mathematics. She herself is a neat person and organizes her world with great care and precision. She favors strongly those children who are also neat and organized. She feels these children make her life easier. "Their papers are easier to correct." But basically she likes them because they possess traits she favors highly in herself. Other teachers like the ambitious, polite, well-mannered student.

Factors we dislike in ourselves can influence our dislike for others. What we reject in ourselves we often strongly reject in others. These factors arouse anger as well as dislike, and they will be considered in great detail in the chapter on anger. Suffice it to say here, many teachers discover that a major reason for disliking a child can be a characteristic in that child that reminds them rather painfully of an undesirable trait in themselves.

The same trait favored by one teacher can be disliked intensely by another teacher. Some teachers prefer persistence, others label this trait stubbornness. One teacher may value flexibility in a child, another teacher may consider it a sign of insincerity. One teacher has a special feeling for tomboys, another obviously favors feminine little girls. One teacher is upset over a boy who plays a great deal with girls rather than with other boys; another teacher encourages interaction between the sexes in the classroom.

One teacher admits quite frankly that he "just can't stand lazy, fat children. It's funny, but it's fairly difficult to restrain myself. I can handle the skinny ones." This teacher knows that a thirty-to-forty-pounds-overweight child needs special help, wants a personal relationship with the teacher. But, "He irks me. I resist, although I shouldn't. I spontaneously go over to the other ones. He'll get it last." This teacher has always disliked fat persons of all ages.

Another source of special teacher feelings is the kind of child the teacher never did like when he or she was a child. Miss Paskin was a quiet, well-mannered girl when she was in school. She rarely misbehaved or spoke out of turn. She caused no trouble for teachers and conformed easily to rules and limits. As a child she severely disliked the children who always tried to get away with something, who deliberately annoyed the teacher, and who enjoyed the times when they successfully "got the teacher's goat." Miss Paskin still dislikes this kind of children when they appear in her classroom. She responds with the same old feelings, becoming at times moralistic and punitive toward such children.

Certain likes and dislikes are generally shared by most

teachers. They are not quite so unique and personal. The child who is responsive to teachers, who obviously likes the teacher, seeks out the teacher, looks up to the teacher with respect, obeys the teacher's authority—this is the kind of child it is hard to dislike. The child easily raises the teacher's own self-esteem, makes the teacher feel important, worthy, needed and, most of all, successful. If a teacher makes a special effort to help a child in a subject, and the child responds by improving in competence, the teacher has every right to feel pleased with himself. And he is pleased with the child, who is both the source and result of the teacher's adequacy and success.

The child who seeks out more knowledge and "has a spark of curiosity" fulfills the teacher's expectations of the ideal learner. Such a child is a delight to teach and shares a special place in the heart of most teachers. Though teachers know at least unconsciously that any teacher could succeed with such a child, they still enjoy such responsiveness and eagerness.

In addition teachers seek out in children different signs of responsiveness and success. One child obviously likes the teacher and shows it by expressing warmth to the teacher. Another child shares his personal feelings with the teacher. A third child responds intellectually to the teacher. Different teachers will respond to each of these children differently. Some teachers prefer closeness and warmth, others feel more comfortable with more distance between them and the children.

Most teachers find excessive dependency especially unnerving. The "clinger" can drive most teachers batty. Miss Roberts has a second grade class. She successfully communicates to the children that she is there to help them, to listen to their problems, and to reassure them when necessary. Deborah got the message only too well. She is a hand-waver, talks a great deal in class, and always wants to tell Miss Roberts what's on her mind. Margery has an opposite reaction to Miss Roberts, which is just as upsetting. She is quiet in the classroom situation but snuggles up to Miss Roberts at every opportunity, follows her about like a shadow, and clings to her skirt and legs. "What should I do now?" "How do you do this?" "I can't make this!" "Help me." These kinds of dependency are especially disliked by teachers who emphasize independence in children (and usually in themselves, too).

The clinging child restricts the teacher's freedom, ties the teacher down to one child. The teacher's own independence is severely limited. The child in turn is exhibiting overdependence, which is usually interpreted as a weakness or sign of immaturity by independence-oriented teachers. Dependence and needing others is devalued by these teachers who advocate independence, self-sufficiency, and rugged individualism as strengths. One teacher reports, "I have always been annoyed with any people who cling to me. I just don't like them."

Some teachers, however, encourage dependence. They especially like children in their classes who respond by leaning on them. Children who appear weak or who call on the teacher for help can make a teacher feel needed, useful, and important. At a crucial point in a teacher's life, this kind of child can help a teacher gain (or regain) a sense of importance or value as a human being. "Someone needs me"; "He can't get along without me, the poor thing" are reactions of parents as well. A feeling of being wanted and needed can play a major part in the teacher or parent's liking for a child. To be able to comfort children, to give them closeness and warmth when they are in trouble, can add immeasurably to a teacher's or parent's feeling of worth. A child who uses teachers in this way can become a very special person in a teacher or parent's emotional life. Of course, at times, this kind of need in the teacher or parent may not foster crucial independence in children. Some children need to cope with their troubles by developing inner resources and strengths rather than by leaning heavily on adults. These children may be hindered in their own growth by the teacher's need to be needed.

The "tattler" has another form of child behavior that can arouse dislike in many teachers. The child who informs on other children, who points out their misbehaviors to the teacher, who "tells," certainly arouses dislike in other children. Teachers generally do not like such children either, even though these children are attempting to please or win the teacher's approval. The "pleaser" is usually so obvious and blatant in seeking the teacher's favor that most teachers dislike such behavior. Most teachers recognize that such children are in disfavor with their peers. Their friendships are obviously weak, their loyalties in serious question. The "pleaser" or "tattler" embarrasses teachers who do not wish to face in themselves the amount of power they possess to favor or approve.

The "quitter" is another kind of child whom certain teachers react to quite negatively. The child who easily gives up causes certain teachers special pain. These teachers value persistence, courage to face failure. Many children give up either because they can no longer tolerate the pain of failure or because they feel dependence on others. Either of these reactions can be interpreted easily by teachers as weaknesses. Some of these teachers recognize that this attitude arises from their own childhood experience. They were made to feel weak, rejected by parents or teachers when they gave up. This kind of child stirs up old memories of failure. Out of a sincere interest in helping this child, this kind of teacher rejects "giving up," pushes the child to try again, and feels dislike if not anger when the child resists, "cops out," turns into a "jellyfish."

The "sneaky child" exhibits another behavior that upsets many teachers. Mrs. Robbins can not bear children who are mousy and sneaky—the child who backs out, lets someone else get caught; the child who blames others or denies his own behavior, his own responsibilities. She likes children who are honest, outright, and open. Mrs. Robbins also feels that girls are more sneaky than boys. Boys, she says, "admit it." They say, "So what, I'm caught." Girls are absolutely crushed and burst into tears. The boys usually repeat their misbehavior, so it is not the misbehavior that bothers her, but the child who is unwilling to admit his faults. Many women teachers feel that boys in general are more direct and open about their behavior. Mrs. Robbins even recognizes this in her own children at home. Her son is more direct, and this pleases her greatly.

The dirty child, the one who smells, the slob, all produce generalized distaste and negative emotions in teachers. Some children, especially from very poor families, bathe infrequently. The resulting body odor arouses feelings both in the teacher and in the rest of the class. The teacher must then deal not only with his disgust and distaste but the obvious and more flagrant reaction of the class. Emotional reactions to the use of toilets also invoke disgust. In classrooms where toilets are in the back of the room, odors can upset the entire class. Children will react outwardly to toilet smells, and if they are identified with one child, that child is in for much dislike. The nose-picker makes many teachers "sick to their stomachs." It's not hard for a teacher to feel revulsion in handling the test paper of a child who a few minutes before was observed vigorously picking his nose.

The "defier," the "smarty" who dares the teacher to punish, and the flagrant "disobeyer" also arouse strong dislike and often anger. This child, who "has to get in the last word," the one "who defies whatever the teacher says," or "who works overtime to do whatever you don't want him to do" is hard to like. Some children deliberately interrupt the class over and over again attempting to provoke the teacher to act toward them. Others pick on other children, seek out their weaknesses, differences, or oddities. Certain children are quite sensitive in discovering the teacher's Achilles heel, then with great skill pick on it, poke at it, arousing much dislike in the teacher. One teacher reports how a child tests out her kindness and sympathy, knowing she is not a strong disciplinarian. Some children have a talent for "making faces" in a way that arouses humiliation and loss of respect for the teacher. Some children mutter inaudibly, but in such a manner that the disrespect for the teacher comes through. The resulting giggles are equally upsetting to inexperienced teachers.

The "liar," the "cheater," and, of course, the "stealer" are also children who arouse dislike. Lying is especially disturbing because most teachers value honesty and sincerity very highly. The child who lies to avoid punishment or never delivers a note sent home to his parents can easily arouse dislike.

Many other kinds of behavior stimulate dislike from teachers: children who are bored, uninterested in what the teacher has to offer; children who daydream and apparently live in a different world; children whose parents have special status in the school system or the community, etc.

Teachers also tend to develop likes and dislikes for groups of children and even entire classes. A music teacher says she feels guilty about stamping an entire class, but, "That sixth grade just isn't interested in music"; "Mrs. Jones's section is impossible"; or, "The fifth grade just hates science." Some groups of children gang up on a teacher. A group of bright verbal boys drives one teacher batty. A clique of girls always giggles together. Their teacher dislikes their entire clique, even though some of the children are "good" kids.

The "blah" kids are basically ignored, neglected. One teacher says, "For some reason I blocked her out. She doesn't interest me. She's not a discipline problem. She's a quiet, little girl. She won't finish her work. She doesn't say much." This teacher feels indifferent to this child. She feels bad that she has not been able to motivate the child, but she herself finds no motivation in herself or the child to act on. Her feelings for this child are dead, nonexistent.

Another significant source of liking and disliking is the economic, social, national, or religious background of the teacher.

We all have special feelings about the religion and nationality to which we belong. Some teachers were brought up with strong attachment to their own group. They are familiar and find great comfort with the language, customs, dialect, and other ways of this group. In addition they have strong feelings about how their own group has been (and still is) treated by other groups. Such religious minorities as Catholics and Jews; such national minorities as Italian, Polish, Irish, all have feelings about their own groups' treatment by the "white Anglo-Saxon, Protestant" majority. Naturally, Negroes, American Indians, Mexican-Americans, Orientals, all have strong feelings about their groups' past (and present) treatment by the "Anglos," the whites, the "man."

Feelings of inferiority and superiority, rejection and hurt, protection and withdrawal, are all part and parcel of majority-minority group relations in our society. The teacher does not shed these feelings when she relates to children. They play their biggest part at the beginning of the school year when the teacher has yet to know each child in her classroom personally. At this time the teacher is more likely to react in terms of her own background and group membership. She brings to the classroom the prejudices and stereotypes that exist in our total society and in her own specific groups. As she gets to know the children in her class, these group prejudices lose much of their influence. They can, however, be rearoused by specific situations.

Miss Kowalski has heard and faced much in her life because of her Polish background. She's most familiar with the hurt of Polish jokes, the humiliation of the Polish stereotype, the "dumb" Pole, and the derogatory feeling attached to the word "Polack." Generally, these feelings in herself, however, have played little part in her adult life. The people she meets, her friends and colleagues, are neither obvious nor blatant in referring to or avoiding this national prejudice about Polish people. Her few Polish friends do provide her with some special comfort as a member of an in-group with similar background. They share some use of the Polish language and, of course, mutual feelings about non-Polish "enemies." Her parents want her to marry someone Polish, but she doesn't consider this essential and has dated many non-Polish boys and men.

One, and only one, child in her class is Polish. Mary, unfortunately, is at times unpleasant, unfriendly, even downright nasty. When these times occur, Miss Kowalski recognizes a rising and old inner conflict in herself: "Why doesn't she behave properly? What will the others think of Polish people if Mary is so mean? Why can't she get along?" Miss Kowalski feels deeply hurt that Mary's unpleasant behavior can be used to support any negative stereotypes about persons of Polish background. At these times Miss Kowalski has special feelings about Mary which are based on their mutual nationality. She may become harsh with Mary in order to show her "how she should behave to be accepted."

Underneath, Miss Kowalski feels sympathy, compassion, and, of course, hurt. At other times, other feelings are aroused in Miss Kowalski. Jokes about religion, nationality, or racial groups will sometimes be heard in the classroom. When the class studies Poland in geography or at the time of a special holiday or when a news event featuring Poland appears in the newspaper are other such occasions.

Special feelings for children can be aroused by meeting

their parents at open house or at a PTA meeting. The teacher may discover that a child's parent behaves, dresses, or talks differently than the modern middle-class, Anglo-Saxon American norm. There may be national, religious, or socioeconomic customs and manners that the teacher finds unpleasant or downright negative. These will be discussed in greater detail in the chapter on parent-teacher relationships, but they do indeed affect a teacher's liking or disliking for a specific child. Sometimes the teacher favors a child whose parents are poor or "old-fashioned." Or the teacher may feel sorry for the child who has to "put-up" with such parents and try to "Americanize" this child into quickly learning middle-class ways and dress.

Teachers are not immune to such terms as *wop, kike, spic, nigger.* They have special feelings depending on their own background and their own adjustment to inferiority, hurt, and rejection based on group memberships. Racial and economic differences arouse such special feelings that they will be considered in a later chapter.

Likes and dislikes also occur due to sexual differences and sexual feelings. Though it may seem obvious, women teachers have different feelings about their girl pupils than their boy pupils; and men teachers feel differently toward girls in their classrooms than toward boys. Parents, too, feel differently toward their own children, depending on the sex of the child. Because so many feelings, in addition to likes and dislikes, are related to sex, the entire topic of sex will also be considered in detail in a later chapter.

How do children respond to a teacher's liking and disliking? Is the teacher's spontaneous feeling something that harms a child?

Many teachers feel quite casual about the effect on children. "It's better for children to know the teacher is a human being"; "children like the teacher to act naturally";

"children would benefit if they were the teacher's favorite."

Some teachers think it is wrong to have likes and dislikes, but they continue to have them, anyway. Many teachers try to hide their spontaneous feelings, usually quite unsuccessfully. At best, these teachers feel that by consciously admitting their feelings, they can effectively treat all children fairly and otherwise give each individual child attention, care, and concern.

A great concern in this regard must be the child who is neglected or disliked continuously. It is hoped that each child will find one teacher (perhaps in physical education, the shop, music, art), or the nurse, who will like him. Or perhaps next year, with a new classroom teacher, he will be more fortunate. However, certain children year after year, teacher after teacher, never click positively with anyone. These children are truly neglected in the educational process simply because they arouse no positive feeling in teachers.

3

The Angry Teacher

IF WE COULD LISTEN IN ON CLASSROOMS WITHOUT BEING seen, we would hear many kinds of anger being expressed by teachers. One teacher frequently screams and yells at her children. Another furiously bangs on his desk. A third teacher throws an eraser across the room. Another sarcastically insults a child. One teacher grabs a child furiously and shakes him. One teacher slaps a child; another raps children on the knuckles. Many angry threats are heard: "I'll show you who is boss"; "Don't talk to me that way." One teacher is furiously tearing up papers, another charges back and forth across the front of the room, letting off steam.

While they are with children, teachers (and parents) do indeed get angry. Sometimes the anger is mild, at other times a raging fury. Some teachers only occasionally get angry, but almost all teachers lose their tempers at one time or another while in the classroom. Their anger may be expressed in different ways, it may vary considerably in intensity, but it is a very real and very important feeling. Anger is crucial to teachers, because teachers must find ways to cope with it while they are in a professional situation. It is also important because adults do not generally like to admit that they get angry. Many teachers (and parents) interpret anger in themselves as a sign of immaturity or weakness. This inevitably creates even more difficult problems for teachers when they are feeling anger.

What Makes Teachers Angry? First of all, anger often occurs as the result of accumulated irritation, annoyance, and stress. An incident, sometimes minor and insignificant, can trigger off what has been building up for many hours or even days.

Mrs. Jones comes to school today a little tense and jumpy. She's had an argument with her husband at breakfast. It wasn't anything she considered serious, but she is not feeling her normal self today. As the morning wears on, she realizes her capacity for understanding children is more limited today, her usual sympathy is missing, and her patience is at an end. Bill and Johnny are talking to each other too often. A child interrupts an explanation she is giving. Several children rough it up with each other while going out to lunch. Each incident seems to increase her inner tension. Once or twice she snaps impatiently at the child, but the anger is kept inside, and she guiltily goes on with her lesson. There's a nagging feeling that her annoyance is wrong, that her husband is to blame, that it is not fair to take it out on the children in class.

Yet as the day progresses, Mrs. Jones's patience wears thin, and her anger reaches explosive proportions. In the early afternoon, Joselyn, who is usually a quiet, well-behaved child, starts buzzing with the girl behind her. She does this during Mrs. Jones's attempt to explain an important point about fractions. This is the last straw. Of all children, Joselyn fails her at a time when she should be most cooperative. Mrs. Jones releases all the accumulated anger that has built up all day. She yells at Joselyn with a voice full of hurt and fury. Joselyn and most of the children are surprised, even shocked. Certainly Joselyn's behavior was not serious enough to provoke such an outburst from the teacher. Mrs. Jones then feels embarrassment, which adds still further to the emotional woes of her day.

Would it have been better if Mrs. Jones had not held in the anger to let it grow and expand all day? Should she have expressed her emotional condition to the class when she came in that morning? Should she have talked to someone, gone to the teacher's room, or otherwise dealt with her anger in some way outside the classroom?

Accumulated anger puts a terrible strain on teachers. In occupations where employees get ten-minute rest periods or coffee breaks, there is at least some opportunity to release pent-up feeling. But a teacher is usually restricted to the classroom and must continuously be responsible for an entire class, hour after hour. She can't daydream, sleep, or otherwise withdraw from the situation—all methods that children, for example, can employ while they are physically forced to remain in the classroom.

A second significant source of anger is any kind of child behavior that arouses in the teacher some dislike for herself. Miss Kowalski often feels anger at Joanie. Joanie is shy, fearful, timid. Miss Kowalski as a child was shy and fearful and even as an adult frequently feels uncomfortable, uneasy, or fearful in the presence of other people. Joanie's timidity and shyness arouse in Miss Kowalski serious and long-standing feelings of dislike for herself. Miss Kowalski has always been unhappy about her own shyness, felt she missed a great deal as a child because of it, and she wishes desperately at times that she was not so timid. She has a generalized negative reaction to shyness in herself and of course in others as well. Miss Kowalski does not want Joanie to have the same problems she feels she has had, and does not want Joanie to miss the fun that Miss Kowalski feels she missed. Her real concern for Joanie gradually arouses long-standing dislike for herself, which spills over into open anger at Joanie.

Teachers, in their sincere concern for children, normally and naturally use their own experience to judge and evaluate the behavior of children. Parents react to children the same way: "I don't want my child to turn out like me"; "I can't stand it when he behaves the way I do"; "I remember how painful it was for me, and I want to spare Joanie that kind of pain."

There are many types of behavior or characteristics of children that remind teachers of traits they are dissatisfied with in themselves. The child who clings to the teacher may remind the teacher of her own overdependence on others. It the teacher feels that her own overdependence on others is a weakness, then she may make strong efforts to remove or stamp out this weakness when she observes it in children. She can only feel anger at a child who behaves toward her in a way which she rejects strongly in herself.

Some teachers are dissatisfied with what they feel is a "bad" temper in themselves. They may have had long-standing objections to their own use of a bad temper as a way of expressing anger. And of course just such a teacher will object strongly to a child expressing a "bad" temper. Ironically, the teacher usually expresses this objection by expressing his own bad temper to the child. "Shut up!" Parents, too, may react strongly against just such traits in their children, attempting to stamp out a bad temper they reject as an unfortunate trait in themselves.

Another major source of anger at children are those types of child behavior the teacher envies. This, too, involves dissatisfaction with the way that the teacher feels about herself. Miss Tannenbaum was never very popular as a child, was somewhat introverted, had few friends, and always envied other children who were outgoing, vivacious, and popular. One of her students, Bernice, is just such a child. She has many friends, she is sought out by numerous children, and her ideas are quickly accepted by her peers. Miss Tannenbaum often consciously envies Bernice, and finds herself getting angry at her and picking at her more than the other children for the same misbehavior.

Children who are obviously and easily successful with the opposite sex can arouse envy in a teacher who has doubts about his or her relationships to persons of the opposite sex. Children who are attractive physically can arouse envy in teachers who possess some negative feelings about their own bodily image. Children who are extraordinarily bright or creative can also arouse envy in teachers. Children from well-to-do families who easily and visibly flaunt expensive possessions can arouse envy in teachers who have a background of meager finances, economic poverty, or stingy parents. The joke about the beat-up old car in the high school parking lot belonging to the faculty, while the newest sports models belong to students, has validity in many suburban high schools. This may arouse envy and anger in a teacher who is struggling financially to support a family on a salary that is considerably lower than those of the parents of the students he teaches.

Certain child behavior is especially effective in arousing in teachers intense dissatisfaction with themselves. Feelings that are particularly unpleasant for teachers to cope with in themselves include humiliation, fear, ridicule, and embarrassment. Mr. Virgil is an eighth grade teacher who prides himself in his ability to handle children, to manage a room full of boisterous, noisy early adolescents. He gets angry, however, at disobedience. A child who flagrantly disobeys, who stands up to him and disagrees, who says "make me do it," creates for Mr. Virgil the problem of humiliation and ridicule. For him these feelings are intolerable. They arouse extreme feelings of dissatisfaction with himself. They imply that he has failed as a teacher and as an adult. He has lost his authority, his control. He fears, moreover, that other children will attempt to disagree, and the entire class will gain the upper hand. He spontaneously responds with anger to any ridicule of his authority. He thereby quickly avoids humiliation by expressing anger toward a child.

Other teachers feel humiliation or embarrassment over their own needs to be perfect. This may occur when the teacher doesn't have the answer to a child's question, when it appears that a child knows more about a subject than the teacher does, or when the class discovers that the teacher made a mistake or gave the wrong answer. At these times most teachers feel a loss of self-esteem, a dissatisfaction with themselves, accompanied by embarrassment. This, too, can be quickly covered up by anger.

Children who mutter, almost inaudibly, insulting remarks, who talk only when the teacher's back is turned, who show lack of interest in what the teacher is offering the class, who ignore the teacher—all can cause anger in the teacher. These children become the target for the teacher's anger, because they cause the teacher to lose self-respect. Basically these responses cause the teacher to feel dissatisfaction with herself, and this self-dislike is directed outwardly at the child who arouses the feelings.

Basically, a teacher's anger toward a child in these situations can often be explained as some kind of dissatisfaction the teacher feels toward herself which has been turned outward toward the child. In some teachers the self-dissatisfaction is strong enough to be self-anger. Since one can only tolerate a certain amount of anger directed at oneself, one normal way of coping with self-anger is to direct it outwardly toward a child. A teacher who is angry at herself because she makes mistakes, because she is not as popular as she would like to be, or because she feels ridiculed when children disobey, usually turns this anger away from herself and directs it outwardly toward a child.

This is, as we have seen, a frequent source of guilt in teachers. "I hate myself"; "How dumb can you get"; "What a stupid thing for me to do"; or more secretly, "There I go again."

Another important use of anger by teachers is to resolve mixed, confused, or ambivalent feelings toward a child. When teachers feel two different ways toward a child, both they and the child are often confused or uncertain. Anger can be a means to eliminate the mixed feeling because it produces a single, strong, negative emotional reaction. Mrs. Angelo finds that on occasion she gets angry at Johnny. Johnny is an outgoing, aggressive, active, and very busy boy, just the kind of boy who represents a masculine ideal for her. She is delighted with this masculine behavior, encourages it both consciously and unconsciously, and is usually pleased with Johnny. At times, however, his behavior gets somewhat out of hand, he gets into fights, becomes more rowdy, and disturbs the class.

At these times, Mrs. Angelo is both pleased and displeased with Johnny. She wants to stop his behavior, but is somewhat confused because she has also encouraged it. Her initial efforts to control Johnny are always unsuccessful because her feelings are so mixed and uncertain. As he continues to misbehave, however, her uncertainty usually reaches a point where she can no longer tolerate it. Her uncertainty, her mixed feelings, her hesitancy, disappear in a flood of anger. In expressing her anger, she finally resolves the confusion of her feelings. It is like the moment of truth, and Johnny always recognizes it by obeying. Anger serves a useful purpose for Mrs. Angelo in dealing with Johnny. It eliminates, at least for the moment, her mixed feelings. It produces the kind of firmness Johnny recognizes as Mrs. Angelo's finally "meaning business," and he responds by stopping his misbehavior.

There are numerous occasions when teachers feel mixed or ambivalent feelings toward children. Since these feelings create discipline problems, they will be discussed in detail in the chapter on discipline. A few illustrations here will demonstrate how important they are in causing anger in teachers. Teachers often have mixed feelings about "special" children in the class—the child who is physically handicapped, the child who has special home problems or is being seen by a psychiatrist, the child who is a member of a rejected minority group, etc. In dealing with these children, the teacher's feelings of special concern, pity, or sympathy are mixed with feelings of annoyance or need to discipline. Here again, as the mixed feelings become intolerable, they are resolved by a sudden expression of anger. Anger eliminates the confusion and replaces it with one strong outburst of negative feeling. Soon after, of course, the teacher may feel guilty for having got angry. But at least during the outburst of anger, the confusion has been resolved, and often to the useful end of communicating firmness to the child.

Parents, too, frequently get hung up with mixed feelings. For example, a parent's feelings of annoyance or a need to discipline may be mixed with feelings of, "I'm a lousy parent," or, "I should be permissive and let the child do this thing," or, "He won't like me if I make him obey." Anger is useful for parents too, because at the moment of anger, all guilt, uneasiness, and doubt disappear.

Anger is normal. Or is it? Anger in middle-class society is decidedly frowned upon. A premium is placed on controlling anger, not showing it, not expressing it. This means, essentially, anger should be hidden, covered up, denied, masked. A person who expresses anger often feels childish, immature. Teachers normally accept these attitudes about anger. They, too, were brought up in our society, a society where, as children, an expression of anger on their part was met by punishment from parents and teachers. Ironically, when children express anger, they meet strong disapproval from adults, a disapproval usually expressed by anger itself. A well-known cartoon shows a father holding a child over his lap and spanking him. The father is saying, "I'll teach you to hit other children."

As a society we are even more confused about anger, particularly the physical expression of anger. Movies, TV programs, and children's cartoons are saturated with physical expressions of anger, especially fighting and killing. Our country uses military means to force and kill others; expressions of anger are condoned in war and so-called police action. Our financial investment as a society in ways of forcing, hurting, and killing others is gigantic at the national, state, and local levels. In the home, parents express anger to children in many ways, including physical punishment. Husbands and wives express anger outwardly and frequently in the presence of children. It is considered legitimate, moreover, to express anger against the opposing football team, the one you would like to see lose the boxing match, or whoever is the latest enemy our country has, be it the Germans, Japanese, Viet Cong, Communists, Hippies, etc.

In terms of frequency of expression, anger is normal. It exists everywhere and is in all of us. But most teachers and parents find it difficult to accept anger as normal and inevitable. The real issue for the teacher and parent, then, becomes the question of how to deal with anger in oneself.

The pressures on us to control or hide our anger are very powerful. Teachers ask, "Will this be held against me as a sign of incompetence or immaturity?" Other concerns are: "What will the kids tell their parents?" and, "Will this get back to the principal?" Teachers, in addition, have real concern for their children: "Will a child become frightened?" "Will it damage him in some way?" or, even more upsetting, "Will the child get angry at me, become rebellious, and no longer like me as a teacher?"

These concerns are so real that most teachers try to hide

their anger. The results of this are quite predictable: At best the teacher who is straining to keep in anger is tense, irritable, and impatient; at worst the anger slips out in sarcasm or explodes in a rage of accumulated fury. Other teachers report headaches, sickness of various kinds, and of course the proverbial ulcers.

Sometimes a teacher may be tense or impatient and recognize only later that the underlying force behind this was anger. Some teachers report that they never get angry in the classroom. In further discussions with teachers regarding situations or behavior which typically arouses anger, some teachers recognize all the signs of anger, but actually did not *feel* anger in the classroom. But usually an observer or the children in the classroom recognize the signs of anger. The teacher was only successful in hiding the anger from herself, not from anyone else. Certain teachers are more successful at hiding anger, but unless anger is in a mild form, it will out one way or another. Because all of us feel guilty about our anger, teachers often engage in a variety of shenanigans to convince themselves or others that they are not angry. They may even make efforts to be especially nice to children they are angry at, and may permit children to behave in ways that are generally objectionable or against the rules, or bend over backward to show the opposite of anger.

One of the major sources of difficulty with anger is the inevitable physiological reaction that accompanies the feeling. When we feel anger, our bodies react with a burst of adrenalin, our blood rises, and our pulse beats faster. Physical tension develops spontaneously, automatically, and without any control on our part our bodies prepare for the "fight or flight" reaction. We need to release this physical tension through action of some kind. But how many opportunities to release physical tension exist while one is teaching a group of thirty-five children? Teachers feel the bodily need to run, bang, even to hit. These are inevitable, spontaneous ways of releasing the built-up physical tension.

How do children react to anger? All of us, as we recall our own childhood experiences in school, can remember instances of teachers expressing anger in the classroom. Though children frequently face anger from adults, they do not always adjust to it in ways that foster their own growth and learning. Teachers report that children often react with confusion; they're bothered, or their faces appear troubled. Some children are especially sensitive and hurt at the teacher's anger, and a few children are even frightened. Sarcasm or biting remarks that touch areas of special concern for children can be remembered with special misery for many years. Teachers who make fun of children, pick out certain weaknesses or deficiencies, make nasty remarks consciously or unconsciously about the ethnic, religious, racial, or economic background of the child can leave lasting scars in a child's attitude toward teachers. Children often feel blamed by the teacher's anger and react by feeling "something is wrong with me." The child's feelings about himself can be dealt severe blows by certain ways of expressing anger.

Usually a child responds to anger with anger. For children, the problem becomes one of how to express their anger to the teacher. Generally speaking, teachers forbid children to express anger overtly to themselves, and so this anger must be expressed indirectly. Children are often forced to express their anger outside the classroom. One summer I worked in a settlement house with a group of seven-year-olds from the slums of Chicago. During the summer these children developed into a cooperative, active, highly sociable group and engaged in a variety of constructive activities. When school began in the fall, they entered an overcrowded elementary school. Some classrooms had forty-five to fifty children, even two children to a seat. Teachers were constantly tense, struggling to keep order, and flaring out with anger. The lid was kept tight on the kids in order to maintain order. Few children expressed feelings in classrooms during the teaching day, and if they did, they were severely punished.

At three o'clock the children fled out of school heading for the settlement house. They burst in each day loaded with anger, energy, hate. My once cooperative, constructive group was almost uncontrollable. The first half hour or more each day was spent in pure release. They were incapable of any constructive activity. From September to June, day after day, children burst out of school as if they had been released from jail. These children never regained the level of constructive activity they had attained the previous summer. Even at the end of the school year they were an angry, sullen group, with needs to hurt each other, to attack, to destroy. The anger they could not release in school was released in the streets and in the settlement house.

Children would like to release anger directly at the teacher. Since this usually results in more pain for the child, children develop indirect ways of expressing anger. Children sometimes become embroiled in learning problems in the classroom as a means of coping with their anger. A child's resentment and hurt can render him ineffective in dealing with academic material in the classroom. He may withdraw from class discussions and daydream. The Walter Mitty type of daydreaming often serves the purpose of providing the child with the fantasies of revenge on an angry teacher. It is no accident that all the cartoons and movies on TV always make a smaller creature successful in beating up a larger, stronger creature. The smaller popeye always beats up the strong man, mice win over a cat, cats over dogs, etc. Children of all ages enjoy them as an opportunity to seek fantasy revenge on all older, stronger, larger, and more powerful adults. Daydreaming in class, lack of attention, doodling, and other fantasy releases are a frequent source of complaint by teachers.

Anger toward the teacher can be expressed by not following the lesson, not turning in homework, and by more direct means such as disobedience, muttering, and the like. Another way of expressing resentment, which is considerably safer than directing it at the teacher, is to start a fight with other children. On days when teachers are angry and upset, they report more tension in children, more fighting, more need for release, and less attentiveness in class.

Especially significant are the indirect effects on children that result when the teacher is struggling with his anger. When under the tension of this struggle the teacher is least able to understand what is bothering the child because he is completely concerned with what is bothering himself. He is less able to recognize subtle clues of child distress, to feel sympathy for a child, and to understand how certain children feel. The teacher's patience is limited, his natural, spontaneous mode of relating is stifled. The teacher is "not himself," and children lose out by not receiving the full potential of the teacher's excitement, concern, and feeling.

Certain children seem little disturbed by the teacher's anger. Apparently they are accustomed to much adult anger and have made their own adjustments to it. It is more difficult to assess the long-range effects of these adjustments. For these children anger does not seem to solve anything. It doesn't clear the air, it doesn't resolve conflicting emotions, it doesn't provide temporary release. It almost appears that the teacher's anger flows over their heads with no reaction.

The teacher faces numerous occasions when anger is normal and inevitable; where fears about expressing anger are powerful and inhibiting; where the effect of the child's growth and learning become a real concern; and where some form of physical release is required.

How do teachers actually deal with their anger? Which

ways are considered best, and why are they considered best? Inevitably, teachers deal with their anger in many different ways, with the wide range of behaviors available to all human beings. They may express their anger in school or save it for an outlet outside their place of work. They may somehow release their physical tensions in the classroom or hold it back until they are out of school where they can really "let go physically." Their anger may explode directly at the child who aroused it or may be displaced toward another person, possibly a loved one, who would more easily accept it and understand it. A great deal of anger is released on the teacher's own family.

Mrs. Levy, a kindergarten teacher, expresses her anger very indirectly. "Johnny, I can't let you play with the blocks now." Translation: "I'm furious, and if he bangs those just once more I'll go out of my mind." Other teachers restrict children to their seats, assign independent work, or in other ways keep children occupied, busy, and hopefully out of trouble.

Mr. Jackson in sixth grade pours on the homework in arithmetic for tomorrow. He's quite angry because the principal just called a special teacher's meeting, and he had planned to go bowling. Bowling provides an outlet to unload his tensions. A few drinks during the evening also help.

Mrs. Jones goes home and yells a great deal at her own children. Another teacher scrubs her floors vigorously, using a special hand wax to polish them when she is particularly angry.

Some physiological release is necessary to relieve the bodily tension built up during anger. Teachers have many ways of attaining this release, even in the classroom. For example, banging on desks with fists, slamming books or rulers, tearing up papers, getting up and pacing around the room vigorously, all help some teachers. Shouting itself provides some physical relief. Getting out of the room whenever possible provides at least the opportunity to walk and certainly removes one from the temptation to hurt a child. Physical restraint of children can sometimes both stop a child from misbehaving and provide the teacher with the physical opportunity to act. When the teacher is angry, the use of physical restraint can border on physically hurting the child. For example, a teacher can dig his fingers in too hard in holding a child, or actually use excess force. The teacher's role in this situation is similar to the policeman's role in using physical restraint.

Some teachers are skilled at expressing their anger verbally without upsetting or blaming a child. "Bobby that makes me angry," or, "I'm mad," or simply, "Damn it." Mr. Bates uses humor when he is angry. He comes in one morning, obviously fatigued and upset, "I got up on the wrong side of my broomstick this morning, kids, so let's take it easy today." This kind of approach can't be used every day, but children will respond to an honest expression by teachers. Sometimes, Mr. Bates gets angry enough to express his feelings, but not so angry that he can't say, "All right kids, cool it, before I blow my stack."

Children themselves can sometimes turn a tense situation into a relaxed one through the use of humor. Children sometimes pick up a teacher's mannerisms, language, or special phrases and use them humorously to release anger and tension. One teacher blasts out the word "zurch" when he is upset. The children in his class quickly caught on. As soon as a child misbehaves, or the teacher's temper appears evident, someone in class yells out "zurch," the kids laugh, joined by the teacher, and the emotional release benefits the teacher and the entire class. Another teacher reported using twenty-five push-ups as a punishment for one older boy who was capable of managing all twenty-five of them. Later on in class whenever another child got sassy, someone would blurt out, "You'd better shut up, you can't do twenty-five." The class would laugh and the situation would be ended.

Teachers also use humor directly. One child in the lower grades always tipped his chair back on two legs, a habit that drives some teachers batty. This teacher was no exception, and she expected the chair would fall over backward at any moment, and the child would bang his head. She was annoyed at the child for ignoring her and finally dealt with the situation by saying, "Paul, would you put all six of your feet on the floor please." The class laughed, and tittered; Paul straightened up his chair. Other teachers report that sometimes a child can make a funny face that is so out of line that everyone (including the teacher) burst out laughing, dissolving the anger.

There are certain kinds of release for anger that teachers consider acceptable and healthy, and that also provide a learning opportunity for children.

Most teachers agree that any anger release that is damaging to children is generally unacceptable. "I always get a feeling of guilt after it"; "I don't like to jump on a kid"; "How would you feel if someone unloaded on you?" The first important criteria of acceptable anger release is that the child not be blamed, attacked, insulted. Second, it is helpful to most teachers if the way they express anger provides some opportunity to release the physiological tension that builds up inside them. To move, to act, to charge about the classroom or school building in ways that are not damaging to children, give the teacher a chance to unload, to let loose, even to explode. There are times when the physical tension "must out" and cannot be ignored. Third, anger that is expressed spontaneously, so that it clears the air, can both remove the tension and the disturbing cause.

One boy in class who consistently belted girls inevitably built up annoyance in a woman teacher. She finally burst out with "cut that out" and he did. The anger was clear, forthright, and effective. When a teacher "really means it," children usually respond. This teacher, after relieving her anger, immediately could revert back to her more "normal" self. She could then be friendly if not warm and helpful to the boy who did the clobbering. By removing anger from herself, and producing an appropriate response in the child, the "air was cleared."

Another teacher reported how the principal charged down to his room one day and accused him of keeping children after class so that they were late to their next class. Since the principal "chewed him out" in front of a couple of other teachers and several students, the teacher was furious. By the next day, he calmed down somewhat and decided to demonstrate to the principal that the children did not have sufficient time between classes to move from one room to another. Previous to this incident, this teacher had never once sent a child to the office for an infraction of the rules. That day, however, he sent all the children who came to class even one moment late right down to the principal's office. He actually sent one hundred eighty-seven children to the office in one day. The principal got the message. Soon afterward, schedules were changed so that children were given more time to get from one room to another between classes. This kind of effective expression of anger was, as you may imagine, immensely satisfying to this teacher.

Fourth, many teachers agree that children can learn some significant things about anger from a teacher who is honest about his own anger. A teacher who faces his own anger and expresses it without damage to children can help children learn to face and accept their own anger. One teacher reports how an especially upset child responded to the teacher's honest expression and discussion of anger by applying it to himself. He did this when he came to class quite upset and angry. At these times the child dealt with his own anger by blurting out "don't mess with me today." Everyone respected his angry mood for the day. Children easily recognize that their own feelings are legitimate in such an emotional climate. "When I'm mad, people in class will treat *me* differently too!"

Developing this kind of sensitivity to the feelings of others is certainly a valuable learning experience for children in the class. Learning to face feelings in oneself and learning to recognize and face feelings in others are lessons that go hand in hand. There is still another potential learning experience about anger for certain children. These children have great difficulty accepting anger and affection in the same adult. For some children an angry, furious adult implies rejection, blame, and that "end of the world" kind of fear. A teacher who gets angry, clears the air, and then is able to be warm and affectionate, teaches these children something new about anger. Anger is not the end of a relationship or a sign of complete rejection. Adults can get angry and still like you. Of course, certain children already know this and sometimes act more "maturely" than most adults. These children can get angry at other children, say the most nasty insults, and ten minutes later be playing happily with them again. Many adults after such a barrage of insults would feel hurt and rejected, and perhaps never speak to the person who insulted them so furiously. Certain children in this sense handle their anger in a more "mature" way than many adults.

Many teachers discover that anger is best released by sharing it with other adults. Many a woman teacher goes home at night, spills out to her poor husband the anger and problems of the day. Often teachers share their feelings with roommates and others they live with. A most useful place for anger-sharing is the teacher's room. This means of dealing with one's feelings will be discussed in considerable detail in a later chapter. Suffice it to say here, however, that the person the teacher chooses to unburden to must be sympathetic. "I know how you feel, that kind of thing drives me batty, too" can provide great reassurance to a teacher that her own anger is not so unique as to be unusual or abnormal. More of this later.

Despite all these positive, helpful ways to express anger, teachers are sometimes going to just plain lose control and let loose their feelings on a child or a class. We all "lose our cool" sometimes. It's perfectly normal, inevitable, and human. If it happens, many teachers find it easy to simply apologize to the children or class at some later time when things have cooled down. Certainly, a teacher should talk it over with someone, in or out of school, who can help her. If she blows her stack too frequently, perhaps she should temporarily leave teaching or even seriously consider another profession. Most teachers can, however, get help from within the school from a school psychologist, counselor, social worker, or another teacher. Some teachers seek professional help elsewhere.

4

Middle-Class Shock

MISS BARNES HAS JUST QUIT HER TEACHING JOB. SHE'S been at it for less than three months, but now even that short time seems like a nightmare. She's been teaching in an inner-city school located in an urban slum. She did not voluntarily choose to work in a ghetto school, but when an opening occurred, she agreed. After all, she loved children, and these children needed help badly. She gave it a try. Although she was not especially enthusiastic about this school, she wanted to succeed and to do what she could to teach and help these poor children.

But she had failed. And failed quite miserably, with humiliation. She could not handle the children. They drove her to tears. She couldn't stand the constant fighting and the destructiveness. Second graders, pushing over desks in anger, seemed an unusually disturbing thing for young children to do. She was brought up in parochial schools where respect was valued very highly, obedience was expected and received, and proper behavior and manners were automatic. She was literally shocked and amazed by this extreme behavior. What shook her up most was the "filthy" language used by such children. Though she had heard some of these obscene words in her college dormitory, no one had ever expressed these words personally to her. And here were little second graders cursing each other out at the drop of a hat, spontaneously screaming out four-letter words, and in front of her, the teacher. Down the hall, five-year-olds in kindergarten were just as sophisticated in their use of obscene language.

When Miss Barnes heard these words, a shudder passed over her entire body. The horror, the shock never ceased. Some of the experienced teachers said they had become accustomed to the language, but Miss Barnes's whole being rejected having to face this kind of experience as a daily occurrence. Other behavior of the children was just as upsetting. Miss Barnes had had it. She quit. She felt a complete sense of relief. It was over. Thank God. Never again.

Miss Barnes is perhaps one of the more fortunate slum teachers. She got out, left the painful situation because her feelings were too intense, too overpowering. Many inner city or slum teachers have similar emotional reactions, but somehow they stay on, survive physically. However, although they are physically present in a given situation, emotionally they are not. Emotionally they are dead. They feel little more than intense stress and pressure. These teachers look forward with great eagerness to the end of the morning, the end of the day, the end of the week.

Middle-class teachers, brought up in middle-class homes, living in middle-class neighborhoods, attending middle-class schools, have carefully and successfully avoided any realistic contact with the slums or with poverty. Occasionally, middle-class teachers may drive through the slums in a car. They usually lock their car doors, look with fear at the lazily lounging adults on the street corners, and with horror at the garbage in the streets, the old, torn mattresses lying in the front yards, the unpainted houses, the slanted porches, the gangs of children loudly dashing about. Newspaper stories of rape, knifings, muggings, add further horror. Television films of riots, burnings, shootings, police and National Guard with fixed bayonets, all do nothing but heighten the middle-class teacher's need to escape the slums, get away, return to the comforting peace of a white neighborhood or suburb. Boarded-up buildings and stores, children dashing into the street with daring unconcern or defiant gestures, hasten the middle-class driver's need to drive fast, flee, get back to the familiar, the comforting, the safe.

Perhaps most frightening is Race. The middle-class teacher in the slums sees all around him only black faces. Rarely does a white person appear. These black faces are at home here. This is their neighborhood, their ghetto, and these are their homes. Probably for the first time the white teacher feels the real impact of race. To be the only white in a neighborhood of blacks, to be in the minority, means facing all the guilt, tragedy, exploitation, horror, and hate of race relations in this country. Whether the community be Negro, Mexican-American, Oriental, or an Indian reservation, the racial separation is strongly evident. The white teacher now feels what he has hitherto been able to avoid: the hate for whites, the poverty of minority groups, the power of white prejudice, the consequences of hundred of years of discrimination, and exploitation.

Working in a school located in such an area means daily confrontation with at least some of the consequences of this great American Tragedy. The evidence in the young, in the child in school, is often less flagrant, less frightening than in the adult from the slum. The school itself frequently becomes a middle-class, if not white, haven in the midst of the horror of the ghetto. But sheltered and protected though the school may be, the children still bring each day to school their scars, their experience with poverty. They bring their customs, their ways, their language; they bring their hurts, wounds, lacks, fears, hopelessness, and their hate.

Much of the behavior of slum children is emotionally upsetting to middle-class teachers. The most disturbing is that which is radically different from the typical upbringing and experience of the teacher who grew up in a comfortable, nonslum home. The slum child's behaviors that are most striking are these related to violence, cleanliness, property, sex, and responsibility. These are the behaviors that usually arouse the strongest feelings in most teachers.

The slum child's need to fight, his ability at fighting, and his style of fighting are often extreme compared to the average teacher's experience. Many children in the slums fight for survival, to protect themselves from others. Children also fight to gain status and prestige in the eyes of their peers. And when they fight with each other, it is a serious business, also a violent business, even in the classroom. Desks and chairs are thrown on the floor, children jump on each other, they scratch, bite, punch, and kick.

The violence and vehemence of serious fighting by even very young children from the slums can be quite shocking to many teachers. "I couldn't believe that children could fight like this. I came from a home where you just didn't fight like that."

Another experience related to fighting, which is upsetting to many teachers, is the way parents encourage their children to stand up and fight for themselves. One teacher reports how shocked she was when in the schoolyard she broke up two girls who were fighting, scratching, and pulling each other's hair. She held one girl back with great effort just as the mother appeared and angrily blasted the teacher. "I want her to learn to fight." The teacher was crushed. All her middle-class sensibilities, her values, her beliefs, were shattered by a mother encouraging a daughter to protect herself by teaching her to fight back.

The school and teacher get into trouble here in numerous ways. The natural tendency of teachers is to break up a fight and discourage children from fighting. The slum strongly advocates the opposite behavior. The teacher's natural, middle-class response is to encourage children to depend on adults to solve their conflicts. "Tell me if he bothers you." "Call the teacher if he hits you." Forget it! In the streets you have to fight your own battles and, especially, not expect adults to fight them for you.

The aggression and habits of older children can be unnerving. They defy adults flagrantly, ridicule and make fun of rules and regulations, and just plain disobey. Teachers report that children who are not in their own classroom can be especially defiant to authority. Dealing with children in the halls, in the playground, or other places outside of school, puts the teacher in situations where she must face children outside of her own group, children who don't know her or participate in any of her classroom activity. These children can and do express their hostility to authority and to whites (if the teacher is white) by letting loose on the teacher.

Another upsetting experience for middle-class teachers is the report often heard on Monday morning of the weekend violence in the ghetto. Knifings and shootings are reported by the children and often verified in the newspapers. The world in which these children live is radically portrayed by violence. Children unfortunately observe this violence and bring to school the residue of hate and hurt. The teacher has to cope with her own horror, fear, and the usual anger—all these are inevitable reactions to the world in which the child lives in between his hours in the nice, middle-class school.

Though we are becoming more accustomed to violence in our society, most teachers' firsthand knowledge of violence is restricted to the television screen, the daily news from Vietnam, reports of the summer riots in the ghetto community, and news of assassinations. Most middle-class adults recognize no violence in themselves outside of an occasional flare of hate. Therefore, they are both unaccustomed to it and afraid of it. The middle class, moreover, channels its violence into indirect, impersonal techniques. Instead of punching a neighbor, we call a lawyer and vehemently fight the battle through the courts. We hire police, soldiers, and others to violently control and kill people we can't or won't deal with.

Violence flares up occasionally in the family, on the job, in the community, but most "well-brought-up" persons live outside this violence, avoid it, condemn it, and rarely experience it personally. The middle-class teacher in a slum school is often frightened, hurt, or angry at being exposed to the violence of life which he has more or less successfully avoided in his own mode of living.

The second pattern of slum behavior that arouses emotion in teachers is that related to cleanliness and property. Many of the children live in inner-city tenements with very inadequate bathing and sanitary facilities, and in overcrowded stituations where maintaining one's personal cleanliness is difficult. Some are recent migrants from rural poverty and have had little experience with overcrowded living and urban sanitary facilities. Middle-class teachers daily face children who are dirty, whose breath and body smell bad, and who wear torn, tattered, and inadequate clothing.

Cleanliness is next to Godliness in our middle-class culture, and there is some question as to which is actually rated more highly. In terms of the amount of money we spend on cleaniness in our society, keeping clean is of top priority. We are deluged daily by TV commercials and magazine ads which successfully convince us that we need soaps, cleaning powders, creams, air fresheners, deodorants, and hundreds of other "cleaning" items. These are all calculated to hide our natural odors and perspiration, eliminating dirt and grime, removing the soot and smell of our polluted air, etc. From childhood we are taught to feel distaste and disgust and even anger when exposed to dirty, muddy, messy, filthy, smelly, and sweaty things and people. Many teachers react with just these feelings to slum children.

If the middle class view cleanliness as almost Godly, they view the preservation of private property as clearly sacred. Tearing books, ripping up bulletin boards, crayoning on walls, cutting up furniture, and demolishing toys and equipment are all considerably more frequent in slum schools than middle-class ones. These acts of aggression are either done violently or casually. Either way they express an indifference to the value of property that can only be felt by angry and hurt children who feel a meager sense of ownership and owning. The destruction of property is highly upsetting to adults who value material things. The middle-class teacher feels a deep sense of hurt and outrage at seeing the signs of his civilization being torn up and valued so lightly.

The young slum child who does not have this sense of ownership does not feel this sense of property, because owning something requires a sense of self. "This belongs to me," requires a firm feeling of "me," of who I am, of who I am not, and of my destiny. Those children in the slums who have no clear feeling of self can have no sure feeling of possession. As soon as the scissors are brought out, they disappear. By the next day eight pairs are gone. The teacher reminds the children to return them, and by the next day twelve pairs are returned! The children are even unsure about what scissors they have or have not taken, or to whom the scissors they see at home belong, or where they came from.

Taking things that do not belong to oneself—sometimes called stealing—is prevalent in inner-city schools. "They carry everything home." "They help themselves!" "They take toys, paper, crayons, etc." Many teachers are incensed by this. They feel angry and even hurt that children could "steal" from them. One teacher was shocked when money was stolen from her purse in the classroom. She knew it had to be some child from her own class and could not believe that one of her own children would do this to her. She was crushed, her feelings of loyalty from the children seemed suddenly illusory. It brought a great sense of relief to this teacher to discover that the child who had taken the money was a child new to her class.

Middle-class teachers can develop strong feelings about children taking things that do not belong to them. In actuality, of course, stealing is not behavior restricted to people from the slums. Evidence of middle-class thievery is more effectively hidden in the crime statistics, but middle-class suburban schools have serious difficulties with stealing, destructiveness, and other such "pranks." Even college students engage in panty raids on co-ed dormitories and are quite destructive in certain other situations. Taking pencils home from the office or samples from the shop is somehow not viewed as stealing, but only because they are engaged in by "respectable, law-abiding" citizens.

Embezzlement is strictly a middle-class crime, engaged in by middle-class citizens in positions of authority in banks, corporations, offices, etc. Embezzlement is a serious problem in this country as upwards of three billion dollars are stolen each year by such "respectable" persons. In addition, one billion dollars is lost each year to employee thieving.

Why then is the middle-class teacher so disturbed and shocked by inner-city thefts and destructiveness? It does appear that much of this outrage and anger is merely a reflection of uneasiness and guilt and unsure adjustment on the part of the teachers. Some teachers admit to a feeling of envy of the lower classes, others recognize the temptation in themselves to behave more freely. Almost all middle-class children steal at some time or another during their own childhood. This is sometimes called "Developmental Stealing" because it frequently disappears. Perhaps it does not really disappear but merely hides below the surface to emerge as punitive anger toward others who are doing and perhaps getting away with what we are tempted, but afraid, to do.

The next area of high emotion for middle-class teachers is the expression of sexual feelings. Sex in the classroom will be discussed in a later chapter, but in the slum school it presents strong emotional problems for middle-class teachers. Slum children often come from subcultures where all feelings are more directly and openly expressed. For these children sexual feelings are directly expressed and in ways usually quite unfamiliar to the teacher. The expression of toilet and sexual words has already been mentioned as a frequent source of disturbance to the teacher. The kindergarten teacher listens in on this conversation: One five-year-old calls another "you faggot." The child asks, "What does that mean?" and a third child quickly answers, "a queer." The teacher is badly shaken; the children go on with their conversation.

Even direct physical expression of sexual interest is expressed in the classroom. It is not unusual for young boys to jump on or mount girls, exhibiting obvious sexual motions. The teacher herself is not immune from this physical interest in sex. Young female teachers have boys following them about the classroom, hands touching their bodies, hands reaching under their skirts, hands between their legs. Even adult sexuality is well known to these children. Children will relate specific details of the sexual behavior they have observed at home over the weekend. Many teachers, especially the unmarried, are shocked and fascinated with these intimate reports.

For most adults any direct sexual behavior is bound to arouse a variety of feelings—excitement, interest, and curiosity, mixed with embarrassment, disgust, and shame, often followed by anger. Sexual feelings, of course, are among the more difficult feelings for adults to adjust to, undoubtedly because they are so mixed with fears and shame. The lower-class child shows considerably less fear and shame regarding sexual matters. Some teachers recognize within themselves some envy of this more open behavior, as they feel uncomfortable about direct sexual expression. The middle class in general tries to hide all feelings, including sexual feelings. The teacher's own effort to hide, cover up, or keep private such feelings is doomed to failure in a slum school, because children so outwardly and physically express their sexuality. And a teacher can be badly shaken up when her personal reactions to sex are aroused in the classroom.

Another aspect of slum life difficult for the teacher to understand or accept is the view of responsibility held by slum parents and children. Mr. Marks teaches third grade in an inner-city school populated mainly by Negro children. He is white, from a white-collar family. He worked hard to get ahead, went to college, surpassing his own father's education. He considers work, responsibility, attendance in school, promptness, and neatness as prime virtues. Retha is a pupil in his class. She is eight years old. She comes from a large family in which her mother is the head of the household. Retha goes home for lunch and each day is always fifteen minutes to a half hour late in returning to school. In the afternoon she is either restless or tired, frequently does not finish her assignment, doesn't seem to care. Mr. Marks labels Retha as lacking in responsibility and makes a comment to this effect on her report card, which goes home to her mother.

The behavior Mr. Marks observed did not fit in his middle-class view of responsibility. If he is interested enough and capable of transcending his own background, he may discover that Retha is not irresponsible at all. In terms of her own life and struggles, she is a most responsible child. Though only eight years old, she goes home for lunch each day shepherding her younger brother, aged seven, and a younger sister, aged six. While walking home, she helps them and herself out of such serious trouble as fighting and such dangers as cars. Once home, she makes a lunch of sandwiches for them, makes sure they eat most of it, and sends them back to school. After tidying up a bit, she grabs a banana and some candy and heads back herself. She usually arrives late after such a busy lunch period. No wonder she is weary all afternoon.

Sometimes such teachers as Mr. Marks do discover how responsible a child like Retha is. Unfortunately, then they often tend to shift the irresponsible label to the child's mother. How could a mother behave so badly, leaving three small children unsupervised. Actually, Retha's mother, rather than stay on welfare, took a more responsible stance. She went out and found work. In order to do this, she had to train Retha to make lunch and watch over her younger siblings. She had to check up on Retha and support her in these responsibilities. This is not an easy task for a mother of an eight-year-old! Most middle-class mothers find it impossible to teach their eight-year-old daughters to even pick up their own toys, much less take care of younger siblings.

Yet, typically, middle-class teachers respond at least initially to many of the slum ways they observe by labeling them "irresponsible." This kind of label usually carries with it strong moralistic tones, emotional rejection, and often anger. Numerous highly toned prejudices emanate from the high position of middle-class virtue, all of which centers on responsibility. The image of the Mexican-American lying in the shade of his large sombrero, sleeping, the easy-going Latin type, whether of Spanish, Italian, or other Mediterranean origins, the lazy, lounging image of the Negro male, the quiet, do-nothing American Indian, all are stereotypes of the poor in this country. All these stereotypes smack of the label "irresponsible." They deny rather flagrantly the causes of poverty, the shame of poverty, the real responsibility for poverty, which lies in our total society. The moralistic, punitive, and smug superior feelings attached to these stereotypes make it extremely difficult for middle-class professionals to work effectively with the poor.

How do middle-class teachers learn to cope with the strong feelings aroused by daily contact with the poor? There are, of course, many kinds of adjustments that teachers make. Miss Barnes, in the beginning of this chapter, escaped—she just plain quit. Other teachers transfer or seek jobs out of the inner city in middle-income or suburban schools.

Unfortunately, many teachers do not leave, but probably should. Perhaps there are no possibilities for transfer, perhaps they need the salary badly. Perhaps, too, they stay on not consciously aware how painful an adjustment they must make, both for themselves and for the children in their classes.

One of the poorer adjustments of those who stay on is the teacher who "gives up." Mrs. Blake has been teaching first grade for many years in the same school. When she began teaching, the neighborhood was a typical city setting. Families were of the working class or white-collar workers; and all were white. As the years went by, the neighborhood changed, first slowly, then more rapidly. Negroes and Puerto Ricans now predominate. The neighborhood has changed, the buildings deteriorated, a ghetto was formed. She is uncomfortable in the old school. She is not at home with the parents or the children who now live here. Much of their behavior upsets her greatly.

When she talks with visitors or other teachers about the

children, she constantly degrades their work, their potential: "There's not much you can do with them"; "They are way behind in reading"; "I have a *few* good ones." She doesn't seem to be aware that the children might understand what she is saying, because she talks about them right in front of them: "He comes from a terrible home situation"; "She clings all the time because she doesn't get enough affection at home." Her general feeling tone in the classroom is negative. She is sarcastic to the children and probably isn't even aware that she is. She is generally "friendly" on the surface, says the right, proper, and positive things, but her total manner is often cold and indifferent. She is especially disturbed by the children taking things home, grabbing things from each other, "stealing" in school. When these incidents occur, she holds on tightly to herself, bottles up her anger in proper surface behavior. She becomes extremely tense and controlling. She severely stops all expressions of a sexual nature. Except for a few children in her class, who both behave properly and are achieving successfully, most of the children are hardly getting by. Many are learning very little. She sees little positive response in the children, only misbehavior, defiance, and withdrawal.

Mrs. Blake is trying hard to stay in the situation, and the few successful children do occasionally give her a warm glow. For most of the class, however, Mrs. Blake has no hope. She has given up. The shock of slum behavior is knotted inside her in a coldness and indifference. This adjustment permits her to talk, walk, sit, and act, but in a manner in which all human interest, excitement, thrill, and spontaneity are nonexistent. She sincerely does not feel much hope for most of her class. She expects they will turn out the way she views most of their parents: on welfare, pregnant out of wedlock, and out of work.

There is stark tragedy in the middle-class professional who has no hope for the poor, who sees no potential in human beings from the slums. Poor children and their parents desparately need hope, need someone who has faith in them in their ability to learn, to move ahead. The school is the major vehicle for upward mobility in our society and when the school gives up, it is hopeless indeed. If the school lowers standards, does not expect much, the child finds it difficult to expect much from himself. Apathy in the teacher breeds apathy in the children.

Mrs. Blake had good intentions. She can teach well under certain conditions. Her past teaching experience in a middle-class setting was most adequate. A teacher, however, requires some response, some sign from the children in order to keep trying, to keep giving of herself. Mrs. Blake gets little response from the children in her class. They show little interest in learning, less interest in her. They spend most of their time fighting, disobeying, acting bored, and they even fall asleep in class. Why don't they respond? Primarily because Mrs. Blake offers little hope, faith, or excitement to respond to. Unfortunately, there is a kind of circular pattern to this adjustment. Mrs. Blake begins to bottle up her feelings, and the children sense her giving up. She, in turn, senses little response in them and withdraws more of her feeling. The result is clear—there is little feeling of hope, inspiration, and faith in this classroom.

Another kind of adjustment teachers make to their emotional shock is in some outward ways less destructive, but in other ways quite debilitating. This adjustment is based on feelings of pity and superiority. "I feel sorry for them"; "Those poor children"; "I want to help them." The teacher feels sorry for these children because he considers them so helpless and weak. People from the slums are viewed as unable to solve their own problems, unsure of themselves, lacking in self-confidence, obviously in need of help. And this kind of teacher adjustment requires that the children and their parents depend heavily on the teacher to give

advice, to tell parents and children how to solve their difficulties. It is the old "do-gooder" approach, which attempts
to do "for people" rather than "with people." The pater-
nalistic attitude here is loaded with feelings of superiority
and self-righteousness. It is just these feelings of superiority that enable those teachers (and other professionals)
who make this adjustment to cope with their own fear,
disgust, embarrassment, and anger. By feeling superior,
the teacher keeps in check the flood of his own disturbing
feelings. By acting on these feelings, the teacher tries to
eliminate the behavior of the slums that is most upsetting
to him. This is the "clean 'em up, and they will become
acceptable" approach.

An outstanding example is Mrs. Richardson, a homemaking teacher. Mrs. Richardson became convinced that the
children in her inner-city school were coming to school
hungry. She felt they were not receiving a full, nutritious
breakfast at home each morning. Some children were indeed hungry by late morning, some tired, and she felt
deeply sorry for the poor, inadequate care she felt they
were receiving at home. Her solution was to involve some
Red Cross and YMCA ladies who were also interested in
doing something for the poor. Together they decided
(without discussing any of this with the parents of the
children) that what was needed was a demonstration
breakfast one morning at school. The ladies who planned
this project had no trouble enlisting aid from surburban
church groups who also wanted to help the poor. Together
they planned, cooked, and served all the first graders a
special breakfast. This breakfast was carefully designed to
include all necessary nutrients, etc.

Mrs. Richardson was delighted with the success of this
venture. The children ate ravenously well. To emphasize
their endeavor, they called in the local newspapers, who
gladly sent photographers and reporters to record this
effort. The next day the newspapers prominently displayed

photographs of young slum children (and all who were photographed happened to be Negro) being well fed by middle-class ladies (all of whom happened, of course, to be white). The photographs carried inscriptions to the effect that these children were receiving a most needed meal, which they normally did not obtain at home. What was most amazing about this experience was that Mrs. Richardson was deeply hurt because the parents of the children were furious with the newspaper reports. Mrs. Richardson had difficulty understanding why parents would mind having their children taken care of so adequately. The fact that the parents were being labeled inadequate and incompetent never crossed her mind.

Foisting dependency on the poor has been a major method for the middle class to cope with their feelings. By assuming superiority and doing things for the poor, the middle-class professional also reduces his guilt feelings about both race and poverty. We can see all around us how this approach has quite expectedly failed to eliminate poverty. And with increased participation by parents in school decision-making, this method will be less available to teachers in the future.

As communities gain control of their own schools, there will be less paternalism in education and more direct participation by the poor. With a great increase in non- and para-professionals in the various activities of education, there will be more planning together, working together, and doing together. This will replace the professionals' past role of planning for, doing for, the poor. Black militancy, American Indian uprising, Mexican-American unionizing—all are efforts at breaking out of the stranglehold of dependency on the middle class.

The shift in feeling and attitude is moving steadily toward recognizing the strengths of the poor. These strengths are mobilized in various self-help and participation activities. The homemaking teacher who calls in the parents of her children to discuss their breakfast needs ends up planning together with these parents a project in breakfast planning, nutrition, etc. Teachers who do this discover a wealth of ideas and suggestions in these parents. In addition, they recognize how articulate and intelligent parents from the slums can be.

Some teachers cope with their feelings about stealing, fighting, etc., by talking them over with the children. By sharing with them, rather than looking down on them. The children are helped to recognize their own strengths and potential. Miss Woods is a first grade teacher. She is a recent graduate, and deliberately chose to work in an inner-city school. She is especially upset by children taking things from each other. Once a child took money from her purse. In these situations her hurt and anger become aroused, but she typically showed it directly with the children, rather than bottling it up inside. "How do you feel if someone takes something of yours?" "What can we do about it, so that we all will have the crayons and scissors that we need to learn?" Mrs. Vanes, too, deals directly with what bothers her most—the fighting and resulting chaos when things get out of hand. She asks her kindergarteners, "How can we go on to first grade if we don't learn?" "Fighting upsets me very much." "Did you like being hurt?" "What shall we do next time if someone hits you?" etc.

Teachers are entering inner-city schools with more past experience with children from poor neighborhoods. Many have taught Headstart programs, volunteered as college students to tutor children, worked in settlement houses or recreation programs. They are increasingly having their practice-teaching assignment in these schools, and after a good learning experience they themselves often choose to teach in the same kind of situation. They recognize the problems of the poor with understanding and compassion;

they have minimal prejudice. Most important they have hope that these children can learn. They recognize the tremendous strengths in poor families because they have come to know some families personally.

They deal directly with their feelings. They often gain a great deal in sharing their feelings with other teachers through group methods, to be discussed in a later chapter. The adjustments they make to their own disturbing feelings are those that allow them to retain the excitement and personal involvement of teaching.

5

The Guts of Discipline

JOHNNY IS A "DISCIPLINE PROBLEM." HE IS IN MISS Cooper's third grade class, and he frequently drives her "batty." He picks fights with other children and talks to his friends when Miss Cooper is desperately trying to hold the attention of the class. He teases other pupils, often does not finish his work. At other times, however, he is friendly, smiling, and cooperative. What especially bugs Miss Cooper are those incidents when he flagrantly misbehaves. At these times, he deliberately disobeys and ignores Miss Cooper's efforts to discipline him.

One of these incidents occurred just yesterday. It was a hot, tense day. In the early afternoon Miss Cooper was explaining a point in Social Studies. Johnny's restlessness broke out in talking, poking, and fussing with the boy next to him. Miss Cooper, already feeling somewhat tired and weary, ignored this behavior. She hoped he would stop and was trying to avoid an incident. Sometimes this works, often it does not. This time it did not. She finally called out, "Please pay attention." Her voice was relatively quiet, mild, and almost vague. Johnny felt no conviction in her tone and carried on as before. Miss Cooper continued with, "Johnny, will you stop talking." Her tone was more insistent, but mixed with pleading and hopefulness. As he persisted, Miss Cooper felt a sickening feeling inside as she anticipated trouble. In the pit of her stomach anger rose. "Stop fooling around." This time the hesitation was clearly mixed with anger. Her anger swelled, mixed with shame and humiliation. In response to Johnny's making faces at her, she burst out, "Once more and down you go to the principal's office." It was almost as if this were just what he wanted. She finally exploded, "Out, out you go."

Miss Cooper cannot understand why Johnny disobeys and refuses to listen to her. She has discussed this in the teacher's room with the art teacher, the physical education teacher, and the lunchroom supervisor. To her chagrin, she has discovered that these adults have little trouble with Johnny. When they speak to him, he obeys. This knowledge merely adds to her sinking and sickening feeling when Johnny acts up. She feels deep in her guts a sense of inadequacy added to the burden of humiliation, even ridicule, as the rest of the class observes her futile attempts to deal with Johnny.

Is Miss Cooper inadequately trained as a teacher? No, she has the same training as the more successful teachers. Is she lacking in discipline techniques or methods? Not at all. Mr. Smith, the physical education teacher, succeeds with Johnny by uttering one simple word, "Stop." And when he uses this straightforward, single "technique," it works. Is her philosophy of education or the classroom climate she creates at fault? Hardly. She is not excessively permissive or severely strict. Most of the children in her class respond readily to her teaching and cause little discipline difficulty.

Just what is her problem? In what ways is she behaving differently than the art teacher, the physical education teacher, the lunchroom supervisor? What does Johnny respond to in these other teachers that he does not react to in Miss Cooper?

Miss Cooper does not realize, nor probably do the more successful teachers, that Johnny responds not to a technique, method, words, or behavior. He is reacting almost solely to the *feelings* felt and expressed by the adults around him. Miss Cooper's insides, her guts, are shaking, scared. Her feelings are mixed, confused. She is hesitant and timid. Her anger is mixed and interwoven with guilty feelings and shame. Johnny senses all this confusion and unsureness. He responds solely to these mixed feelings. He doesn't really feel she means it, because she doesn't. He even takes some delight in shaking her up.

Mr. Smith, the physical education teacher has a completely different gut response to Johnny. He has no hesitation about discipline. His insides are sure, clear, and confident. In one word, *stop*, he communicates to Johnny the firm feeling that Johnny immediately responds to. The feelings that Mr. Smith has when Johnny misbehaves are a completely different set of emotions from those of Miss Cooper. Johnny in turn responds exclusively to this difference in feelings.

Often teachers and parents recognize that a child behaves quite differently in the presence of one adult compared to another. Often a father can obtain obedience instantly with a specific child, while a mother's attempts result in continued misbehavior, arguing, and anger. Sometimes a mother is more effective in handling one of their children, while a father flounders in indecision and uncertainty. One teacher says of a specially difficult child, "He only responds to the paddle," while other teachers never use physical means on the same child. They have discovered the child responds readily to verbal efforts. One principal insists that "with this kind of children, you must use physical punishment." Another principal takes over the same school, never once uses physical means of punishment, and the children behave as well or better. The difference here is not in the technique. It is solely in the *feelings* of the adult.

Talking with teachers and parents, in courses and faculty meetings, at the PTA, and in a variety of other situations, the topic of discipline is the most frequent one raised. In questionnaires given to teachers and teachers-to-be, discipline appears as a persistent problem, a perpetual headache. For inexperienced teachers discipline rears its ugly head as *the* prime source of anxiety. Teachers and parents phrase their problems many different ways. "Discipline is my biggest problem"; "giving children proper discipline"; "handling children who create discipline problems"; "the greatest problem was achieving and maintaining discipline"; "dealing with tantrums and rebellion"; "bad behavior and conduct . . . noise"; "inattention"; "day to day discipline"; "I want children to respect themselves and others"; "children are difficult to manage"; "getting them to obey someone other than their parents"; ". . . the same thing over and over again."

Discipline also raises many questions for teachers and parents: "What degrees of punishment should I inflict on a particular child?" "How can I get his cooperation?" "How do I keep order?" "How do you discipline children who are not used to discipline?" "How do you deal with fighting, excessive talking, rebellion, dishonesty, stealing, testing out children, belligerence, destructiveness, swearing, etc., etc.?" "When should I limit him?" "How can I punish her and not feel guilty?" "Am I too cruel and insensitive?"

Discipline arouses strong feelings. "The most disturbing thing last year was imposing discipline." "I least like having to discipline children." "The least enjoyable part of teaching is my own lack of patience." "I most dislike imposing arbitrary limitations on a child's development." "I dislike imposing limitations on turbulent children." "I don't like to discipline children." "I feel it wrong to be dictatorial." "It may sound foolish, but I get frustrated and annoyed when children are thick-headed." "It is impossible to teach in the midst of anarchy." "I spend an undue amount of time on discipline." "Children tend to regard me as a peer rather than a disciplinarian." And, of course, there is the frequent, "That kid is driving me batty"; "He bugs me"; "I'm going out of my tree"; etc., expressed in many ways and varying emotional language.

Teachers and parents have many feelings which greatly affect the discipline relationship between them and children. First, there are feelings of uneasiness, guilt, and wrongness. Mrs. Stein is very sensitive to the feelings of children. She readily identifies with them. She senses easily when they are hurt, frustrated, and disappointed. She does not like to be the person who causes this disappointment. Mrs. Stein recalls rather vividly her own hurt and frustration as a child. She feels deeply the disappointment and limitations imposed on children by adults. She feels a sense of wrongness, of guilt when she herself has to be the agent who limits children. The very idea of controlling others makes her feel like a dictator, an old-fashioned autocrat, an overstrict parent. She believes in freedom, creativity, and minimum adult restraint. She believes this because adult control arouses in her the troubled feeling of wrongness.

Many teachers are like Mrs. Stein. They may have had overstrict parents and recall with great feeling their own hurts as a child. They swore to themselves that when they became parents or teachers, they would never treat children in a similar fashion. These adults feel great pain when they discover themselves yelling at a child or preventing a child from doing what he wants to do. Inevitably, they must learn to deal somehow with their troubled feelings, because children must be limited.

The second set of feelings aroused in adults by their disciplining of children arises from the parent or teacher's need to be liked by children. Miss Wiley likes little children. She is warm and affectionate in her dealings with her kindergarten class. In turn she expects and receives many positive reactions from the children. They talk easily to her, they seek her out, they ask for help, they hug her. Miss Wiley, however, feels troubled over discipline, because she wants children to like her. When she limits children, she expects that they will dislike her, get angry at her, reject her, turn away from her. And sometimes they do. If they do, they usually regain their positive mood quickly. Rarely do they remain sullen, angry, or rejecting for long. Nevertheless, Miss Wiley is troubled because she fears the rejection, the sullenness, the dislike.

Miss Wiley realizes at times that she seeks a great deal from her job. She seeks human warmth and affection from her children. She gets considerably less warmth in relationships with adults and frequently turns to children as if for comfort and reassurance. Since she requires this kind of response from children and does not feel she can obtain it elsewhere, she is troubled when children reject her. And reject her they do when she must limit them, stop them from doing what they want to do, or require them to sit quietly, line up, or show proper manners. Many teachers gain these same satisfactions as Miss Wiley does in working with children. Many parents seek a positive, liking response from one or more of their children. When this adult need is powerful and the anxiety of rejection is high, then discipline problems inevitably are created for the adults.

Next, many teachers, and parents too, discover that their own feelings of competence and adequacy are tied to their success in handling, managing, or disciplining children.

Mr. Blake prides himself on his ability to handle children. The principal frequently assigns the children who are discipline problems to his class. He feels that a teacher should be a strong disciplinarian and that learning to behave is crucial in growing up. He is quite successful in managing even the most difficult children. Occasionally, however, a child "gets to him." When this happens, Mr. Blake becomes quite upset. A child who disobeys defiantly makes Mr. Blake feel ridiculous and humiliated in front of the class. He fears that others will get out of hand if he shows softness. Mr. Blake recognizes that his feelings of competence as a teacher are determined to a great extent by his success as a disciplinarian. When he is unsuccessful, he feels a sense of failure. Fortunately, he rarely feels this way. But underneath is always the fear of being exposed as weak, inadequate, and even incompetent.

Teachers who frequently struggle with discipline often have powerful failure feelings. Miss Vohns taught in an inner-city school for three months. The children were wild, destructive, and frequently fought violently with each other. Her efforts at discipline were frequent, her success minimal. She quit her job because her feelings of failure as a teacher were caused by her failure at discipline. Most human beings can only tolerate a certain amount of failure feelings in a situation before they too "drop out," and remove themselves from the situation that arouses the feelings of failure and inadequacy.

Because of the variety of feelings aroused with reference to discipline, the teacher or parent frequently becomes entangled in a mixture of feelings. This maze of emotion, when sorted out, usually includes mixed and opposite feelings, which merely heighten the adults' confusion and uncertainty. In turn, the child senses this confusion and uncertainty as a lack of firmness. In the face of such vacillation and confusion, the child typically continues to misbehave. When the adult is able to settle the uncertainty, to feel clearly one way or the other, the child will usually respond to this clarity or singleness of feeling.

Very often, then, when children continue to misbehave or disobey, it is because the teacher or parent has mixed, opposed, or confused feelings.

Mrs. Hart is a fourth grade teacher who feels that teachers should like all the children in their class. Unfortunately, one of her children aroused her instant dislike. He is Perry. Perry can be quite mean to other children, picking on their faults and weaknesses. He teases others and drives some girls to tears. He also tends to blame others for starting the trouble he gets into. Mrs. Hart's dislike for Perry was obvious from the beginning of school. Since she feels she should like all her class, she feels guilty about her dislike for Perry. She bends over backward to be nice to Perry, but, underneath, her feeling has uncomfortably remained.

When Perry flagrantly teases Sally in the hall, Mrs. Hart's feelings quickly flare into anger. Her spontaneous reaction is to pounce on Perry and demand immediate obedience. Underneath this quick reaction, however, her uneasy guilt flares up. Perry senses in her a confused feeling. As Mrs. Hart calls out, "Perry, stop that teasing," she emanates a tangle of feelings—anger mixed with guilt, sternness mixed with uneasiness, sureness confused with ambivalence. She has many doubts about disciplining him. "Do I pick on Perry so much because I dislike him?" "Does he misbehave because he senses my dislike?" "Would I react to a child I liked in the same way?" Mrs. Hart feels two opposing feelings—a need to stop Perry quickly, but also guilt for disliking him. Perry senses she doesn't mean for him to stop, and he takes the next opportunity to poke at Sally again.

Mrs. Hart has got to clarify her confused feeling before Perry will clearly comprehend what she is saying. She must resolve her ambivalence into one straightforward feeling. As was discussed in the chapter on anger, this resolution can be achieved through a blast of anger which clears both the air and Mrs. Hart's mixed-up insides.

There are numerous other reasons why teachers have mixed or ambivalent feelings about a child. In most cases where these mixed feelings are present in the teacher, they are the cause of discipline failure.

Mrs. Jacobs at times finds herself in a situation where she has a need to discipline Gertrude for her misbehavior. Gertrude, however, has cerebral palsy, and though her handicap is relatively minor, Mrs. Jacobs and many of the children feel uncomfortable in Gertrude's presence. They feel sorry for Gertrude because she is crippled, a loner, and because Gertrude makes them feel uneasy. Mrs. Jacobs sometimes recognizes a feeling of guilt in the presence of handicapped persons. She has fleeting feelings of, "Thank God, it's not me," and immediately covers up such momentary thoughts with guilt and uneasiness. When Gertrude misbehaves, Mrs. Jacob's first reaction is to treat her like other children. However, accompanying her need to discipline Gertrude are the feelings of pity and guilt. Her response to Gertrude is mixed, she lets Gertrude get away with many things she would not let other children get away with. Gertrude, therefore, becomes a discipline "problem" at least partly because of Mrs. Jacobs's mixed feelings.

Teachers feel sorry for children for reasons other than their physical handicaps. Children who are members of minority groups that have been discriminated against in our society can arouse such feelings in teachers. This can result in a teacher bending over backward to avoid conflict and discipline trouble. A child who has a psychiatric problem or who is receiving psychotherapy may be treated with "kid gloves" by a teacher who feels sorry for him. Children from a poor family situation or broken home can be pitied. The occasional child who is beaten at home or otherwise mistreated can also arouse feelings of pity in teachers. In many of these cases bad discipline situations can result because of the teacher's mixed feelings.

Another source of mixed feelings that contributes to discipline difficulties is the teacher's fear. A teacher may desire to discipline a child, but may be fearful of repercussions from adults. "What will the principal think?" or,

"What if his parents find out?" can easily hold back a teacher from disciplining a child. Fear of disapproval if parents report a discipline incident to the principal can arouse fears of losing one's job, receiving a bad report in one's record, or not being advanced to tenure, etc. Another source of fear is the child whose parent is a big shot in the community, whose father has a lot of money, or a position of high status either in the school system or elsewhere in the community. Imagine the poor teacher who has in her class the son of the superintendent of schools, and must discipline this pupil! Her feelings are inevitably strong. She cannot easily be casual and natural with such a child. Fears of the possible consequences can easily result in a teacher's feeling both a need to discipline a child and a need to hold back her discipline.

Mr. Stephenson is fearful of another kind of repercussion. He teaches a slower class of eighth grade mathematics, and some of the boys are quite large physically. Mr. Stephenson is not especially tall, never went in for athletics, and avoided physical conflict as a child. He has a great deal of trouble with Ben, who hates math and is a tough kid. Ben likes to show the other boys that he is a leader. Mr. Stephenson is fearful that Ben someday will do this by standing up to him and defying him. They have come close to this several times, but Mr. Stephenson has avoided such a confrontation up until now by giving in to Ben, bypassing him, not expecting as much work from him. This teacher is afraid of a direct conflict because of a real and powerful physical fear of being hurt in a hitting or pushing battle. He is, of course, also fearful of the ridicule he would feel as a consequence of physical conflict between Ben and himself. His fear causes a vacillating discipline, which Ben inevitably takes advantage of.

Miss O'Hara has a related inner fear. Twice she has been confronted with a child having a temper tantrum. The violent screaming, thrashing, kicking, and banging were very

upsetting to Miss O'Hara. In both instances she was im-
mobilized. She didn't know how to handle the child. She
was embarrassed and humiliated. She fears a repetition of
this kind of situation. Two children in her class disobey
frequently and seem to ignore her efforts at discipline. She
is afraid that both of these children are capable of raising
quite a big fuss if she gets too strict with them. Her need to
discipline them is always accompanied by fear of the consequences—fear of these two children acting up and of her
own embarrassment of fear and failure.

Occasionally a teacher is afraid of his own anger. Mr.
Gregg, a seventh grade teacher, rarely blows up, but when
he does, he lets loose. As an adolescent he really hurt another boy in a furious fistfight. Once he broke a door, slamming it so hard in anger. Rick is the kind of kid who de-
lights in getting the teacher in a tight spot. One day Mr.
Gregg had had enough and blurted out, "That's it, down to
the office." Mr. Gregg was furious. Rick, however, sat back
casually in his seat and calmly answered "make me." Mr.
Gregg was raging inside. He really wanted to go up to
Rick, yank him out of his seat, and drag him down to the
office. But the fear of his own anger was overpowering. He
was concerned that he would smack Rick and really hurt
him. Mr. Gregg's feelings were frightfully mixed—a desire
to discipline Rick, and an intense fear of doing so. Mr.
Gregg stamped out of the room to cool off, before he could
deal with the situation. Rick misbehaves, at least partly,
because he knows he can arouse such a fear in Mr. Gregg.

Likes and dislikes can feed additional mixed feeling into
a discipline situation. As in Mrs. Hart's dislike of Perry, a
teacher can feel guilt over disliking a child, which can
interfere with a need to discipline the child. If the dislike
is caused by a prejudice or a personality trait the teacher
dislikes, this can create havoc inside the teacher's guts.
"Am I punishing him because he deserves it or because I
dislike him?" is a real cause of inner distress and often
results in continued misbehavior.

The teacher who likes a child may have her own hang-ups with this child over discipline. She may be hesitant about disciplining the child because she is fearful of the child disliking her. She may not wish to risk losing the affection of a special child. At the same time, she may feel some guilt about having special feelings for a child. The resulting conglomeration of feeling that is expressed when the child misbehaves is easily felt by the child as confusion. And again, many children will in the face of this unsure, hesitant discipline, continue to misbehave.

Another major source of confusion for the teacher in discipline is the feeling of responsibility the teacher may feel for having contributed to the discipline situation. Miss Lark teaches third grade. She has had an especially rough year, with several personal crises, including problems with her landlady and the death of one of her parents. She has not been her normal self this year, and she knows it. She feels a sense of responsibility about how these personal problems affect her teaching and especially how they affect the children. Every once in a while she feels ready to blow up at a child who gets out of hand. At these times, she stops what she is doing, slowly counts to ten. While counting, she carefully considers what is going on inside herself, "I was up late last night, unable to sleep. It's not really the child's fault. It's my fault." Whenever she feels guilty about her impatience and anger, her discipline is greatly weakened. Often she clears up her own feeling and deals with the child more calmly. But at other times the guilt and anger predominate. Then the child reacts to the inner confusion, and a more difficult discipline situation is created. Usually Miss Lark then has to blow up to clear up both her own insides and the tense air in the classroom.

Mrs. Brown has a similar difficulty. Though she has taught for several years, this is the first year she has taught fifth grade science. She never felt very competent in science, but she was needed desperately and finally agreed.

She has taken a refresher course and works very hard at preparation. She is slowly gaining confidence and familiarity with science materials, but it is still not comfortable for her to teach. She relies heavily on her preparation. Occasionally, because of other pressures, she gives less time to preparation and does a poorer job. On these days she feels less confident and even guilty for not being prepared. Jane, a student in her class, has a great deal of trouble with science and acts up when she can't understand what's going on. Mrs. Brown feels uneasy about punishing Jane because she feels that Jane's misbehavior is partly her own fault rather than the child's. On those days when Mrs. Brown is poorly prepared, she has especially mixed feelings about dealing with Jane. Mrs. Brown wants to yell out to Jane to stop talking to her neighbor, but at the same time she feels guilty. Jane senses the confusion in Mrs. Brown and usually reacts by fooling around even more.

Sometimes a teacher has mixed feelings about discipline because he doesn't really believe in the rules or regulations he has to enforce. Mr. Casper supervises lunch period for the children. The principal has a regulation that during lunch the children are not allowed to talk. The lunchroom is small and crowded, and the rule does help keep the busy place from becoming a madhouse. Mr. Casper thinks this regulation is ridiculous. He himself likes to make dining a social affair and enjoys talking with others while eating. He likes to make friendly talk with the children during their lunch period, rather than hover over them as a watchful guard or policeman. He identifies readily with the children, feels their need to talk. At the same time he has been instructed to keep order in the lunchroom by enforcing the rule against talking.

Mr. Casper cannot enforce this rule clearly and confidently. He communicates to the children his tacit approval of their talking. While he supervises lunch, therefore, it is never completely quiet. Mr. Casper's mixed feelings are easily sensed by the children, and they respond to his feelings rather than to the principal's rule.

A teacher can feel sympathy for a child, which can in a similar way result in disobedience. Sometimes teachers recall that they themselves acted the same way when they were children and as a result can't quite develop serious feelings about discipline. This encouraging and/or discouraging of behavior in a child is easily sensed by a child as not sincere. Occasionally a teacher may even gain vicarious pleasure from observing a child defy rules, while he as an adult is incapable of resisting authority.

Some recent student rebellions in colleges have been tacitly, if not outwardly, encouraged by certain professors. At the same time, these professors themselves have strongly felt their own conformity and submission to the authority of law and order. They are incapable of personally defying the college administration, but partly encourage or unconsciously support students to rebel against the same authority. In the student rebellions, these professors gain vicarious satisfaction through seeing the "hated" administration under direct attack. The professors chafing under administration control are in one very real sense encouraging the students to express the very things they feel, but are fearful of saying. This position, needless to say, contributes to student disagreement with authority whether at the college, high school or elementary school level.

Mixed feelings in teachers and parents can create a circular pattern of discipline vacillation. Alex is a boy of eight who is accustomed to varying discipline at home. Sometimes his mother punishes him for misbehavior, sometimes she shies away from it. She is quite mixed up inside about discipline for many reasons. She feels guilty and wrong when she pounces on Alex. Alex, therefore, has learned that at least some of the time when mother says "stop," she is not really sure and clear in her feelings. He learned that about one-third of the time "stop" doesn't really mean stop. His mother will not enforce her discipline. With these odds, any full-blooded American boy is going to keep misbehaving every time his mother says "stop." Each time the odds are good that she will back away, and he can continue whatever he is doing.

Alex has Miss Verone as a teacher. Miss Verone has some of that special sensitivity to the hurt child that has been discussed previously. She identifies readily with the frustration and disappointment of children who have been restricted and limited by adults. She quickly feels the hurt of punishment by an adult and feels bad when she has to be the person to arouse such hurt. On a typical rough day Alex starts out asking if he can go across the room to borrow a pen, which she permits. He can at times be quite charming, too, which makes it more difficult to say *no*. Then he wants to work with George in the back of the room. Miss Verone doesn't really want Alex wandering around, but she gives in rather than disappoint him. When she gives in, she feels some resentment inside herself, but her need to avoid hurting Alex takes precedence. She is irritated, however, when Alex moves about, interrupting her lesson, interfering with other children.

After three-quarters of an hour of this, Alex has three or four children together in a little group of their own, and they are having a big time of it. Miss Verone's patience is at an end. She screams out at Alex with anger, "That's enough. Back to your seats!" She immediately feels guilty for having let loose on Alex, knowing full well she had permitted him to do what she really did not want him to do. She feels terrible inside for having screamed and already has a need to "make it up" to Alex.

He quickly gives her the opportunity. "Miss Verone, may I go down to the library and look up a book?" Miss Verone senses herself falling into the same trap again. She doesn't want Alex to leave, but gives in because she feels so guilty about screeching out at him. Alex leaves for the library. Miss Verone feels resentment building up inside, and off we go again. This *giving in when you feel guilty, and then getting angry* sequence can go on all day, with the teacher building up more and more anger, and at the same time, more and more guilt.

Parents who are home with children all day readily fall into this circular trap. It does not require that the parent or teacher give in frequently, only that they give in when they feel weak and guilty inside. Some children are especially skilled at arousing adults' feelings of weakness and guilt. Direct approaches are sometimes outstandingly effective—"You don't like me!" or, "You let Barry do it, why can't I?" or for parents, "You love Joanie more than me," etc., etc. At the same time adults have many mixed and confused feelings for children, they inevitably have many valid and strong needs to discipline children. Teachers and parents sometimes lose sight of their own needs in the face of all this confusion.

Miss Jones has a third grade class composed principally of boys. They are active, busy, noisy, and aggressive. Most of the time this lends excitement and interest to her teaching. Inevitably, it also becomes wearing. Then Miss Jones feels irritable, impatient, and tired. In the late afternoon Miss Jones feels that the children usually become too tense and tired to work effectively without a rest period. She insists that each child put his head down on his desk, and for five minutes relax without a word. This five-minute break is sometimes difficult to maintain. Certain children just don't feel like resting at this time of the day. Miss Jones, however, is convinced that "it is good for the children to get this rest." At the same time, Miss Jones rarely considers that this five-minute break is extremely helpful to her personally. She benefits greatly by having a quiet time with no hand-waving, calling out, or activity. She herself desperately needs a quiet, passive opportunity to catch her breath, to regain her usual calmness and control. If she admitted her own need for rest, she might have less difficulty getting all the children to respond. It is easier for children to obey a teacher if the reason is an honest one. Even if she approached them with "we all need rest now," it would be more honest than "you need a rest."

Many parents, too, are afraid to recognize their own needs for discipline. They try to convince the child that discipline is solely for the child's good rather than for the parent's well-being. With younger children, certain parents have a great deal of trouble getting them to go to sleep at night. They insist that the child needs to sleep, it is good for his health and well-being. "The child needs ten hours of sleep"; "The pediatrician says he should sleep"; "You need the rest." Some parents are able to be quite honest about it, "I'm tired, you go to bed!" Then the parents can quietly read, talk, or watch TV to regain their own sanity and repair their own psyches. Who really needs the *rest*?

When you consider the emotional world of the adults who live and work with children, discipline takes on a new purpose. It is not solely for the child, for his good, for his growth and development. It is completely valid to consider disciplining children in order to help the adult deal with his own emotional turmoil. Disciplining children can restore a parent or teacher's warm, affectionate feeling which has been swamped in irritation and anger. Disciplining children can restore an adult's intelligent reasonableness, which has become lost in a maze of confused and opposing feelings. It can in effect help an adult regain the kind of sanity that can easily be lost after many hours of contact with the inevitable noise, activity, defiance, and excitement of childhood and of learning.

6

Surviving the First Year

"THE FIRST YEAR WAS HELL. I COULDN'T BELIEVE IT."

"I didn't know what I was getting into. It was horrible!"

"You struggled. You never knew if you were doing the right thing or not. You know, it was ghastly."

"I wondered if I ever taught them anything. It was all discipline problems. I got desperate. It wasn't for me. I just wasn't doing a good job."

"I was full of misgivings. There were constant self-doubts. It was hell."

"The days were more bad than good. You wondered whether you were really cut out for it or not."

"It was sink or swim. That was horrible. Things were completely meaningless."

"I lacked confidence. Deep down inside I was scared. I was downright burning inside."

"Something was wrong with me. My discipline was going all wrong. I decided my class was not responding."

"I was totally up in the air about how to handle them. I felt hopeless and miserable."

"Will they ever learn? Will they ever change? Will things get better? I had constant doubts."

"Most days it was just useless. I was just a referee. What am I doing in teaching?—nothing!"

"I was terrified. I could have lain down on the floor and cried."

These quotes from experienced teachers as they look back on their first year of teaching verify that for many, their beginning year is a living hell. For many new teachers the first few weeks, the early months, in fact the entire first year, is one horror. The feelings aroused are powerful. They are among the most painful human beings can face: feelings of failure, hopelessness, and abnormality. After four years of college training to become a teacher, it is extremely painful to face the realization that all this preparation had led one to a job that is full of frustrations and dissatisfactions.

The feelings of failure are the strongest. Few new teachers feel any success in their teaching, and most feel the intense failure that results from the awareness that children are learning but little. Teachers feel desperately inadequate to cope with a variety of child behavior, and this adds further misery to their feelings about themselves. Self-doubts are numerous. "Is there something wrong with me?" is a frequent question raised with oneself. Only later, by the second year or so, does this question change to, "There's nothing wrong with me. It's the kids (or the principal, or the teacher the child had last year, or the parent, etc.)." School psychologists report that few new teachers refer "problem" children for special help during their first teaching year. One of the reasons given as an explanation is that during the first year they feel they themselves, rather then the children, are the real problem.

Not all teachers, of course, go through this kind of first year, but unfortunately many do. There is a very high turnover in teaching in this country, and because the numbers are so high, new teachers' distress affects many persons.

The number of teachers who enter teaching a year is astoundingly high. Approximately 200,000 new teachers enter the public schools each year. If even a small percentage of this large number find their first year so difficult, then a large number of persons—teachers, children, and parents—are exposed to emotional turmoil each year, just because of first-year survival problems.

Of the 200,000 new teachers entering the schools each fall, approximately 140,000 are hired to replace teachers who left teaching for a variety of reasons. There are, of course, many reasons why people leave teaching. It is difficult to estimate the effect of teachers' dissatisfactions on this high turnover figure. But certainly many of the 140,000 who leave each year do so at least partly because of the problems in surviving with professional satisfaction.

It is doubtful that any other profession has such a high percentage of new entrants each year. The 200,000 new teachers represent over 10 percent of the total persons teaching in public schools. This means that approximately half the teachers now teaching in our nation have taught five years or less. The adjustments that inexperienced teachers make to their emotional problems are therefore of vital concern to children, parents, and educators.

Why is the first year so hellish for so many teachers? The new teacher is inevitably inexpert and unskilled in many ways—discipline, planning units of teaching, presenting material. Feelings of inadequacy about this lack of experience are healthy and productive. It stimulates a teacher to learn, try out new things, seek help, and evaluate his performance. The feelings of inadequacy that are most destructive are those arising from the myths discussed in Chapter 1. To try to be what one is not, to try to feel what one does not feel, to try to hide what one is, places the new teacher in a particularly miserable state.

These myths inevitably plague new teachers much more

furiously than the experienced teacher. The new teacher has little experience of his own against which to test these myths. He has been led to believe that they are correct, that they represent an accurate portrayal of how he should act and feel as a professional teacher. The inexperienced teacher is immediately confronted with his own new and raw experience as a teacher. When his own teaching does not fulfill the expectations of these myths, there are really only two alternatives available. He can assume that the myths are invalid, or that he is failing to live up to them because of some deficiency in himself.

Many new teachers assume the latter. They do not yet possess the inner strengths required to reject the voice of the external, professional authority. Instead, they reject the reality of their own experience and interpret their contribution as failure. Many teachers recognize that they are afraid to behave the way they would naturally like to behave. "I was scared to discipline the kids"; "I didn't know if you could hit the kids"; "I was told to be very strict, to not smile at the children." This fear of being themselves, accepting what is necessary for their own well-being, forces many new teachers into sheer immobilization. Desperate feelings of wanting to escape, to quit, are frequent. The inner conflict can become unbearable.

Student teaching experience can sometimes lessen the emotional conflict resulting from this initial confrontation, if the student teacher is in a school similar to the one the teacher is assigned the first year. This often gives new teachers a valuable learning opportunity. If the master teacher is willing to share her own real, initial teaching experience with the student, this can reduce some of the heightened emotion of new teaching. The new teacher can feel fewer fears about his own "normality."

Sometimes observing a master teacher is valuable, not because the inexperienced teachers learn new techniques during the observation, but because they actually observe a successful teacher doing many things "wrong," "incorrectly," or more honestly. The observing teacher reports, "I felt good to see the demonstration teacher doing the same things I do," or, "She's not perfect either. When she got angry at a child, I felt great." Master teachers can be supportive, positive, and reassuring. Unfortunately, they can also arouse the student's fears and negative feelings. "The new teacher lectured to the children all day. It was terrible." "She made me write, rewrite, and constantly revise units." "She wouldn't let me freely interact with the children."

Many teachers complain, "If anything went wrong, she was right there to step in. I never had the opportunity to deal with crises and with trouble." Another complaint was that university or teachers college laboratory schools were extremely poor preparation for later work in a regular school situation. Most of these schools had so many adults present in the classroom that children rarely were unattended or had the opportunity to misbehave.

Students who have had extensive experience with children before or during their teacher preparation often gain the experience necessary to deal with emergency problems. Many students have been camp counselors, Headstart aides, have taught in Sunday school, done extensive babysitting, or otherwise gained valuable experience testing out their own feelings in actual experiences with children. These students are less vulnerable to the power of the unrealistic myths, because they have the reality of their own experience as an inner resource to counter the impact of the myths.

Teacher preparation can be helpful, too, to the extent it offers an honest, real view of teaching as opposed to the "fantasy" of teaching. Many teachers, as they look back on their college preparation, have very strong feelings about the unreality of their training. "It was very idealistic"; "I was fed up with classes my senior year"; "Things were completely meaningless"; "I didn't get anything"; "I would never go to —————— College again or send a child of mine to that school"; "The courses were all way out."

Preparation that seemed most helpful were those opportunities where students could participate and thereby try out their feelings. In some seminars students were permitted and encouraged to express their opinions and feelings. Specifically, they were able in these helpful situations to talk about their own actual experience with children and relate it to theory, research, and other nonpersonal sources of knowledge. The source of much personal anguish for teachers is their inability to integrate the intellectual and theoretical offerings of the college with the feelings, opinions, and ideas which they themselves developed out of their actual contact with children.

The preparation course most often pointed to as responsible for this inner conflict in the new teacher is the course labeled appropriately "The Theory Course." Teachers looking back on this type of course most often feel considerable resentment. "All the nice little things you learned in college just don't work"; "The theory course was all wrong"; "From the course I didn't know what I was getting into."

For many teachers the training that was to prepare them to teach children and handle a classroom was most unsatisfactory. The training failed them, and the feelings aroused as they tried to apply the training were sometimes overwhelming. Added to these preparation problems, many new teachers feel that in hiring new teachers administrators take advantage of their innocence. Because they are not sophisticated enough to know what problems can be avoided, they are sometimes given especially trying and unusual assignments. "I always had the bus duty." "I got the worst kids in the fourth grade." "It was the lowest group." "We had to eat lunch in the classroom." "They put thirty-six kids in my class the first year"; etc., etc. As the first year wears on, many new teachers supplant their feeling of abnormality with the realization that their situation is abnormal. New teachers often feel that administrators "pour it on." One important thing the new teacher learns the first year is just what questions to ask before he accepts his next teaching job. As a brand new teacher just out of college, many teachers asked only a few basic questions, like what salary they will get, and what grade level they will teach.

Failure, fear, depression, abnormality—how do new teachers learn to cope with such feelings? How do those who experience the first year as a painful ordeal survive? What devices, techniques, mechanisms, do they employ to deal with such overpowering feelings?

The teacher must cope primarily with a host of inner struggles and conflicts between himself and others, conflicts between different feelings and opinions within himself. "Should I be myself or try to please the parent?" "Should I behave naturally or seek the approval of the principal?" "Is my own experience valid, or is the theory course valid?" "Is there something wrong with me, or is there something wrong with the children?" "Should I admit my mistakes or cover them up?" "Am I abnormal, or is this situation all wrong?"

The strengths to engage in the process of seeking answers to these conflicts arise out of the very deep being of the teacher. The courage to discover oneself, to be oneself, exists within all of us. The teacher whose first year is a living hell usually goes through the painful ordeal of self-evaluation and self-discovery. The successful result of this ordeal for the teacher who survives is greatly increased self-awareness and self-confidence.

Though the struggle be an inner one, the outside world makes its contribution to the teacher's efforts. The principal and other supervisors, fellow teachers, and the children and their parents all can either add more fury to this inner battle or assist the teacher in gaining some self-confidence and competence. The major helpful role that others can play is to provide support, reassurance, and direct assistance.

Unfortunately, such supervisors as principals, consultants, etc., are viewed by teachers as offering support only rarely. Usually they are insufficient in number to visit the new teacher frequently enough. Some supervisors do visit new teachers frequently, but they handle their visits by offering "constructive" criticism. This is typically felt by the new teachers as "plain old criticism," whether offered constructively or not. Feelings about supervisors will be discussed in detail in a later chapter. Supervisors can, however, help the new teacher when they honestly share some of their own teaching experience rather than give suggestions, advice, or criticism.

Miss Hanson was a new third grade teacher. It was October. She was flustered and frustrated. The children did not seem to be learning. They did poorly on tests, and many did not answer well in class. Miss Hanson talked to her Elementary supervisor. Instead of giving her more advice on how to teach or going over her lesson plans, this supervisor merely related her own experience. She recalled how every September she felt the terrible frustration of having to start with a new group of children. In September she was a little scared, a little excited. Many a night she couldn't sleep. The future supervisor asked herself over and over again, "When will they ever learn?" By looking back at her old class of the previous June, she recalled how much they had learned since September. She realized she could go through it all over again, and they could learn. Miss Hanson, too, was having similar fears at night. Her supervisor's personal disclosure was very reassuring. When June came, she, too, realized that her children had in fact made considerable progress.

Principals and other supervisors assist greatly when they are able to relieve a new teacher of a particularly troublesome child. They are of help when they can provide teachers with an opportunity to leave the classroom when the teacher cries out for a chance to get away. Sending children down to the office can be of considerable help to a new teacher when she "is at the end of her rope" with the child and nothing seems to work. To eliminate the source of such trouble when the teacher can no longer behave reasonably provides the new teacher with an opportunity to regain her composure and her sanity. The focus of the disturbance is removed, and the teacher can move on to other, less emotional tasks.

A major source of support to new teachers is other teachers. For the most part, teachers help each other on their own, informally and outside of the regular meetings and committees established by the school administration. "My husband was a teacher. He encouraged me." "Most of the veteran teachers were very good to me." "I talked with my roommate." In the teacher's room during lunch, other breaks, and after school are opportunities grasped by new teachers to ask, "How do you handle —————— ?" "What do you do about —————— ?" Over and over again teachers seek from each other specific suggestions, techniques, and methods for coping with daily occurrences. In addition, teachers often share with each other their more upsetting feelings. By disclosing to each other their own fears, inadequacies, miseries, and concerns, they readily discover that most reassuring of all feelings, "Other teachers feel that way too," and, most deeply, "I am not alone!"

New teachers help each other with direct assistance too. They will help out by taking a particularly troubled child from another teacher, by exchanging reading groups, by taking over someone's class so that they get a most needed break, etc.

Children, of course, can provide a most refreshing and welcome support to the inexperienced teacher. When children respond to the teacher, when they spontaneously express positive feelings, when they behave well, when they solve some of their more trying problems, the teacher inevitably begins to feel success. Success, of course, reduces inadequacy and failure feelings, and slowly builds up confidence in oneself. Young children express their feelings more directly. "I love you, Miss Barnes," offered spontaneously in the midst of apparent chaos is particularly heartwarming. "You're great, I will miss you." "We missed you when you were sick." Remarks like this, notes written by children, and gifts offered by children are all evidence of positive, successful response.

Parents also offer real and spontaneous praise, which can assist a teacher in gaining a more balanced perspective about her success and her accomplishment. "Our young daughter will be in third grade next September. Can we ask that she be assigned to your class?" "You just go right ahead and punish him. We are right behind you all the way." Less obvious expressions of feeling are expressed through tone of voice, cooperation in sending to school materials the teacher asks for, and help in attending field trips, etc.

The inexperienced teacher with some support from the outside world reaches down into the depths of her own misery and says, "I'm going to make it. I am not going to quit. I'm going to get to those kids. I am going to stand on my own two feet." This inner strength, this courage, growing out of helplessness and fear, develops an experienced, confident, and feeling teacher.

7

The Principal:
Whose Side Is He On?

ONE OF THE CRUCIAL SOURCES OF FEELINGS FOR TEACHERS are those adults in authority in the school. These inevitably include the principal, but also the assistant principal if there is one, supervisors, and others who are in the organizational structure as persons in authority. Sometimes this includes persons who are not in the hierarchy in terms of their position, but nevertheless are seen as authority figures because of their relationship with the principal or because they have power over teachers. Sometimes a nurse or a custodian or a secretary can wield power in a school way out of proportion to the definition of his job as stated in the organizational structure.

For all these persons the teacher has special feelings— the feelings all human beings have toward persons who are in authority. For children the prime authority is the parent or teachers, for workers their boss or foreman, for all of us the policeman, judge, or any person in a high position of power.

Power is wielded by authority persons in two primary and potent ways—by controlling others and by evaluating or judging others. The principal is the primary administrator in most schools, and he exercises controls over many aspects of the teacher's life. Usually he is also the most important person in the entire school system who evaluates and judges the teacher. The principal, moreover, is not the only authority who both controls and evaluates the teacher. He usually shares this authority with others. Central office administrators establish certain controls over the teacher (when classes begin and what is taught in third grade Social Studies, for example).

Other persons also exercise control over the teacher. The superintendent of schools, the board of education, and others set rules, limits, requirements, and thereby exercise their control.

With reference to evaluation of the teacher, the principal also shares this authority. Central office supervisors frequently influence the principal in his evaluation of the teacher's performance. Ratings of teachers for salary increments, merit raises, tenure, or just for the teachers' personnel files are also made by these supervisors, with the principal.

The teacher may even see the parents of the children in her classroom as a judging or evaluating authority. The teacher's relationships with parents, however, will be discussed in a later chapter. Here we are concerned with the teacher's feelings about those in the school system who exercise control over the job and those who evaluate job performance.

The amount of control exercised by the principal and supervisors affects the teacher's emotions greatly. Miss Green likes to run an informal classroom. She feels she is quite responsive to the moods and needs of the children in her classroom. As such, she likes to plan flexibly. She changes her plans as the children seem to need a change, or as she herself senses a need for something different. If the children are restless, she might like to show a film rather than hold an arithmetic lesson. If they are full of energy and spirit, she prefers taking them out in the playground for some active play, rather than keep them tied down to the four restricting walls of the classroom. If she feels there is more need for socializing, she breaks up her class into small groups, and they vigorously discuss issues in social studies or the literature they have been reading.

Mr. Hanlius is the principal of Miss Green's school. He is a well-organized person. He likes to know where things and people are, so that he can put his finger on a situation if need be. He schedules movie projectors and films at least one week in advance and keeps a large chart in his outer office which quickly and clearly shows the disposition every hour and every day of each piece of audiovisual equipment assigned to his school. He also schedules in advance the use of the playground facilities, and a large schedule book in his office must be filled out at the beginning of each week by any teacher who wishes to use the playground. He is proud of his organizational ability and rightly so. When someone visits his school from the central office or from another community, he knows just what is going on and where. He never has supervisors from "downtown" telling him about things going on in his school that he did not know about in advance.

Inevitably, Miss Green and Mr. Hanlius clash. She feels he is overcontrolling, an autocrat. She feels her freedom is limited too severely. She sometimes feels hurt by his ignoring her flexible point of view about teaching. She more often feels anger. Miss Green must cope with her feelings about Mr. Hanlius and hopefully in a way that they do not spill over into her teaching. The principal's control can operate differently depending of course on the unique personality of the principal. Mr. Hanlius is very controlling about activities that go on outside of the classroom or that affect the operation of his office. However, he does not interfere greatly in the teacher's freedom to teach as she likes within the four walls of her classroom. She can be strict or more permissive, follow a lesson plan precisely or loosely, as she pleases. He considers the classroom the teacher's own domain. However, when the teacher moves out into the halls, lunchroom, playground, etc., he sets up the rules of operation and organizes the use of facilities as he sees fit. He is controlling in one area, considerably less controlling in another area. Some teachers prefer more freedom in the classroom, some prefer more direction. Other teachers, like Miss Green, would like more say in the use of out-of-classroom facilities.

Mr. Kiech is a new teacher who is feeling great anxiety because he has received little direction from the principal or other supervisors. He does not know if he is covering the material as fast as he should, or too fast. He is not sure how much he should expect the children to learn. "Am I being too strict or too lenient?" He would like more control from his supervisors. In effect, the principal gave him the key to the classroom and said "go ahead," without any more specific guidance or direction. He is floundering because of lack of control. Another teacher, as we have seen, might react quite differently to this loose control. Some teachers enjoy this kind of freedom. They develop their own teaching pace and pattern. They set their own standards; they are more comfortable with freedom.

The principal's control can operate in other areas of the teacher's life and greatly affect his emotions. The way the principal uses faculty and committee meetings tremendously influences the feelings and morale of teachers. Miss Greg feels that "too much time is spent on committees." In observing one of their committee meetings, the source of Miss Greg's feelings becomes clear. This is a committee on "report cards" and it has been given the task of evaluating the current report card and making recommendations. The principal would like the ideas and suggestions of the committee members and has communicated this to them. The teachers, in turn, are delighted, at first, to have the opportunity to express their complaints about the report cards and to make the changes they feel are necessary. As the meetings wear on, however, it becomes increasingly clear to both the principal and the teachers that the principal is unable to give the teachers complete control over deciding what the new report card should be like. Comments from the principal like, "The assistant superintendent favors achievement scores. I think we should have a citizenship type of rating," and, "The parents have told me they want written comments" begin to make it clear that the principal is not offering or surrendering very much of his control to the teachers. The principal must deal with the opinions and requests of the assistant superintendent, parents, and others beside the teachers. Perhaps he gave them the wrong impression in the beginning about how much control they were going to have over the ultimate report card. In any event, the revised report card coming out of this committee looks a great deal like the one the principal favored. Miss Greg is furious. "They never give you credit for what you know. There is no freedom of speech." Another teacher says, "Our judgment is not respected at all." The general feelings of the teachers are, "No one will listen"; "We are not appreciated"; "Meetings are stupid"; "Committees don't do anything"; and "We do all this work for nothing."

Some principals are more autocratic than others and control a great deal of the teacher's activity both inside and outside the classroom. Other principals try to be more democratic, but find that giving in to pressures from top administrators or parents is a more powerful need than letting teachers have the say in decisions. The whole area of decision-making in schools is a crucial one in arousing feelings. Teachers feel a great deal of resentment, anger, and bitterness if their views are not considered. They feel pure fury when their views are sought, asked for, requested, and then ignored, rejected, set aside, in decisions that affect their working lives. Assignments, use of facilities and equipment, getting assistance from specialists, scheduling, report cards, and meetings and committees are all areas where teachers have opinions and views. The manner in which their opinions are dealt with greatly affects their feelings of freedom and of control.

Problems of control and freedom are powerful in affecting the teacher's psyche. In addition, teachers must also face persons who have responsibility to judge and evaluate their teaching effectiveness and job performance. Miss Cook is an elementary supervisor who must visit all teachers who are not yet on tenure at least twice each school year. She tries to plan her visit so that she can observe the inexperienced teacher over a fairly long period of time in order to obtain a fair view of the teacher's performance. She always lets the teacher know in advance when she is coming, even though she realizes this usually heightens the teacher's anxiety and sometimes results in the teacher putting on a special display just for her sake. She feels this is still better than coming in unannounced, which can shake up some teachers badly.

Mrs. Hicks is in her second year of teaching. She received a fairly average rating her first year and is looking forward with mild trepidation to how she will be rated this coming year. She did not sleep too well the night before Miss Cook's visit and was quite grouchy at breakfast. When Miss Cook arrived, Mrs. Hicks was teaching a reading group, and the rest of the class was engaged in independent work at their desks. Miss Cook sat in a corner of the room, note pad out to record her observations and comments. As she noticed Miss Cook with pencil poised, Mrs. Hicks felt her heart jump to her throat. The children were already somewhat tense that morning, probably reflecting their teacher's anxieties.

Mrs. Hicks regained some of her composure and went on with her reading group. In a few moments, however, Jimmy grew tired of working on the ditto on his desk and opened up the hinged desk top. He then noisily and vigorously emptied all the books, papers, and assorted junk from his desk, dropping everything on the floor with a bang. He was obviously taking this opportunity to clean out his desk. Piece by piece he picked up items from the floor, looked them over carefully, eventually throwing most of them back in the desk. Occasionally an item seemed worthy of being thrown away, and he would get up from his seat, walk slowly but noticeably to the back of the room, and toss it in the waste basket. On the way back, he would briefly talk to a friend he was passing or point out something from his pile to someone else.

During this performance Mrs. Hicks attempted to work with the reading groups, although more of her eyes and ears were attuned to Jimmy with an occasional glance at Miss Cook, than were attending to the children she was teaching. She was acutely sensitive to how Miss Cook would react to and interpret Jimmy's behavior. When the children left for lunch, Miss Cook in an attempt at reassurance said, "They are an active class, aren't they?" This merely raised Mrs. Hicks's fears.

During lunch the supervisor and teacher talked about the observation. Needless to say, Mrs. Hicks did not enjoy her food, and her digestive system seemed full of growls and cramps. Though this supervisor mentioned many positive things about Mrs. Hicks's teaching, there were other less positive comments as well. When their conference was completed, Mrs. Hicks felt reasonably good about herself as a teacher, but was emotionally exhausted. This was, indeed, and often is, a trying experience for the teacher and the children as well.

Miss Cook did not openly reveal to Mrs. Hicks her emotional reaction to Jimmy's behavior. Probably her feelings about this kind of behavior were not too strong. Sometimes supervisors are less able than Miss Cook at hiding from the teacher their immediate gut reaction to what they observe. Some things they see appall them, other observations arouse disapproval and others negative interpretations. Certain supervisors would quickly interpret Jimmy's behavior as an example of poor discipline on Mrs. Hicks's part. It is likely that this interpretation would eventually find its way into Mrs. Hicks's personnel file. Through tone of voice, facial expression, or choice of words, supervisors often communicate how horrified, shocked, disappointed, etc., they are about a teacher's performance. Sometimes this gut reaction to what is being observed is more successfully disguised, but the teacher senses it and knows well of its existence.

Being evaluated arouses strong feelings for most adults. After years of almost continued evaluation by parents, teachers, and college professors, all adults learn various kinds of adjustments to being evaluated. These adjustments serve the purpose of helping us deal with all the feelings and fears that are aroused when someone judges us. Feelings of failure and inadequacy are unavoidable. Frequently, too, there are feelings of hurt and shame; feelings of being rejected and alone, and of course that most useful of all feelings, anger.

Our feelings about ourselves are very sensitive to negative evaluations from persons in authority. Our self-feelings may be shattered—our self-confidence shaken, our liking for ourselves dissolved and replaced with self-hate, self-dislike, and self-dissatisfaction. Though most adults most of the time do not experience this range of feelings, under the surface these feelings certainly linger. They are hidden, covered up. When they are aroused by a negative evaluation, it shocks us to discover their continued presence. Many adults can recall such feelings from the distant past of childhood, but to become aware of their presence in the here and now can be an emotional blow.

Our adjustments to authority are not always made easily and comfortably. Most adults recognize in themselves, sometimes with great pain, a desire to solve this problem by pleasing the authority, doing what is requested, obeying, conforming. To please the authority assures one at least of an absence of disapproval. Sometimes by conforming, one gains rewards, approval, and praise. Some teachers, as some children, make special efforts to conform and to please. This frequently results, however, in inner conflict and stress. Unfortunately, conforming provides a tempting opportunity to give up the battle for selfhood; to deny one's self and become what someone else wants you to become; to lose one's own feelings, ideas, and uniqueness.

It is difficult to say which adjustment has the more tragic consequences—the teacher who desperately tries to be what he is not, to conform to the authority, and who succeeds at it, or the teacher who tries with great effort and fails at becoming what is expected by the authority. In either case there is an inner battle with inevitable consequences. The teacher loses spontaneity and excitement. While he is trying to please someone else, he is no longer propelled by his own curiosity and interest in learning. By-products, of course, include tenseness, impatience, and anger. Outlets for such tension are required. They may be released outside school or at home, in not too different a fashion from the way people behave in that old joke about the boss on the job bawling out the father. The father comes home and snarls at his wife, who screams at a child, who hits his younger brother, who, perhaps finally, kicks the dog. Teachers also have an outlet in the sanctity of the teachers' room or lounge. Often principals deliberately stay out of the teachers' room so it can be a haven for teachers. Some teachers make a regular habit of getting together socially to release these feelings. The faculties of many schools have adopted favorite bars, where teachers get together, often weekly on Friday after school, to share their feelings and struggles with authority as well as other job stresses.

Direct rebellion is rare as a form of adjustment. It is more often disguised in disagreement and arguing with authority figures. Some of the "hidden agenda" in faculty meetings includes teachers fighting back at the principal and the principal attempting to defend himself.

More often teachers develop, sometimes with great skill, a kind of compromise with authority. This is the kind of adjustment to authority where teachers comply in public and disagree privately. This "surface compliance" has been used by many persons in subordinate positions—children, employees, patients in hospitals, minority group members, etc. As James Baldwin aptly put it, "The Negro learned to tell the white man what the white man wanted to hear." When you give the impression of agreement with the authority, he "climbs off your back," and you are free to think and feel what you wish. You may even be able to act freely, if you don't get caught. This is where the skill is required. Phil Silvers, in a popular TV show, was admirably talented in the role of a sergeant who used this adjustment. He publicly agreed with his superior officer, but privately disobeyed numerous rules and regulations of Army life, often quite flagrantly.

In schools this approach has been aptly put—"Many great things go on inside classrooms that central office supervisors don't know about." And the clincher, "The reason these things go on is because the supervisors don't know about them." Many changes are made outside of the principal's area of control. Some teachers, as mentioned previously, will shift children from one room to another to

assist each other. Sometimes a child is permanently transferred by teachers themselves, without the office knowing.
Teachers have exchanged their reading groups on a regular
basis, worked out team teaching of various kinds, all on
their own.

In one school a group of brand new teachers, all of
whose classrooms were close to each other on the same
corridor, banded together. First they discovered their commonalities. They were all new teachers and all about the
same age. Next, they shared their feelings, concerns, and
joys by meeting regularly almost every day for lunch. They
met in one of the classrooms and ate sandwiches they
brought from home. They talked, and talked, and talked.
Soon they started making plans. They were fed up with
one of the regulations regarding the use of some learning
equipment. One of their group had gone to the assistant
principal and got what he considered a runaround. So the
teachers as a group met with the same assistant principal.
The force of numbers paid off. They got the desired
change they wanted. One of the teachers also wanted a
child moved out of his classroom. The child was a slow
child who really belonged in a special, slow classroom.
There was a lengthy procedure to follow, forms to be filled
out, etc. The person in charge kept saying, "Let's wait to see
if things get better." The child did not do better and still
no transfer. Fortunately, the teacher who taught the slow
class happened to be a member of their lunch group and
agreed to take the slow child. Without the office knowing,
the child was moved, and it worked out very well. Several
months later, carrying anecdotal records and test scores,
the teachers involved went to the "office" and proved the
success of the change. At that point, the office, bowing to
the power of success, gave approval for the change.

Teachers are no different from other human beings in
their desire to participate in decisions affecting their situa-

tions. Student protest on campuses has a similar motive—more student participation in decision-making. Political protest usually has the same force behind it—the bitter, angry mood of a group that feels disenfranchised from governmental decisions. Teachers, by organizing in unions and teacher associations, are asking and even demanding more say in decisions affecting their jobs. By organizing together, by displaying unity in their action, teachers can wield considerable power. In many schools teachers are not only demanding higher salaries, but are demanding through their organized groups a voice in educational policy. Control is inevitably being shared with teachers. This kind of united action has raised considerably the self-esteem of teachers as well as their public image.

Supervisors often try to provide a climate for growth so that teachers may work toward "teacherhood." Sometimes a supervisor deliberately sets a climate where admitting problems and feelings is acceptable. "In this school, you have got to have problems or something is wrong with you!" or "The only teachers here who don't have problems are the liars, and lying is a serious problem!" If this attitude toward having problems is sincere, teachers will be able to use supervisors for help, because they will be able to admit they have problems.

Some school systems attempt to reduce this fear about admitting difficulties by having a special supervisor who is not part of the administrative line of command. This special supervisor plays no role in judging or evaluating teachers. It's safe to talk to such a person. Confidence is respected. Sometimes a school psychologist or school social worker plays this kind of role for teachers. It can be very effective in opening up the channels of learning for the teacher who is fearful of evaluation. Otherwise, conferences can become boring dialogues between a supervisor who asks, "How are things going?" and a teacher who repeatedly and defensively responds, "Everything is fine." This seems safe and sometimes it works.

An unusually sensitive patient in a mental hospital discovered this technique in dealing with authority. Each week the patient's psychiatrist had a conference with the patient and started out asking, "How are things?" For many weeks the patient sincerely responded with a flood of concerns, anxieties, and problems. At the end of each conference the patient asked, "When can I be released and go home?" and invariably got the answer, "Well, let's wait a while yet." After several months the patient discovered how to be released from the hospital—don't share your real feelings. To the weekly question, "How are things?" the patient shrewdly gave the answers called for: "Much better!" "I feel good," etc. His real anxieties and feelings he kept hidden. After adopting this new role, the patient was in fact released as cured of all his "feelings and problems." Some teachers also seek this kind of cure, and some are successful at achieving it.

Inside the relative privacy of his classroom the teacher has a great deal of opportunity to teach as he sees fit. Many teachers do just this. If necessary, they adjust to supervisors by readily agreeing with them publicly and then proceeding to teach the way they want to anyway.

Such surface compliance, when it is used, is not always rebellion. It is often a sincere attempt on the part of the teacher to discover for himself what he is, what he does well, what works for him, what does not, what he can tolerate, what bothers him most, etc. In this process of discovery the teacher learns a great deal about himself and develops his own values and judgments regarding himself and teaching. Since this can rarely take place in isolation from other teachers or from parents, there is little likelihood the teacher will "go off the deep end."

The more teachers meet together to share their experiences, with the assistance of supportive supervisors, the more meaningful the growth process is for the teacher. Supervisors are becoming increasingly aware of the value of this discovery process and the role they have to play to assure its success. In this direction lies the means by which teachers can obtain help in dealing with their feelings—the process of self-discovery leading to real teacherhood.

8

Colleagues:
Friends or Foes?

MRS. ATKINSON HAS BEEN TEACHING FOR SEVERAL YEARS. Her third grade classroom is located partway down a fairly long corridor. Across the hall from her room is another third grade class, and two other sections of third grade are further down the hall. She frequently sees children from the other third grades in the hall and often hears teachers and children in their normal business of everyday teaching.

Mrs. Atkinson spends a disproportionate amount of her introspective time comparing herself with the other third grade teachers. Miss Vane across the hall is outgoing, vivacious, almost bubbly. Her children are often laughing and always seem to be enjoying themselves. Miss Tyler down the hall is very well organized, she runs a "tight ship." Her children are quiet and well behaved when in the hall. The sounds Mrs. Atkinson hears from Miss Tyler's classroom are the orderly voices of one child or the teacher speaking one at a time.

Mrs. Atkinson does not feel that she runs a classroom in the same way either of her two colleagues do. Her children laugh occasionally, but are not outgoing and active. They are neither well controlled nor well mannered. When she hears a burst of laughter from across the hall, a tinge of pain passes through Mrs. Atkinson. "Why are they having so much fun over there? Why are my children so lacking in joy and in laughter? What's wrong with me?" When she takes her children to lunch or to the door to leave, she feels another pang. "Why do my children fuss so much in the halls, poke each other, get out of line? How does Miss Tyler keep her children so orderly?" Mrs. Atkinson often feels uneasy in the presence of these two teachers. As she compares herself and her teaching with each of them, she feels something lacking. And unfortunately this lack seems to be a serious deficiency in herself. "Why can't I be like those other teachers?"

Mrs. Atkinson avoids socializing with the other third grade teachers. She will deliberately sit someplace else when they are in the teachers' room, and if she cannot avoid speaking to them, she talks of materials, equipment, or nonschool matters. She reveals very little of herself. She prefers, in fact, to hide what she considers her true self, an inadequate person, from these two teachers whom she considers "ideal" and "perfect."

Feelings of jealousy are not unusual in teachers. The grass often "looks greener on the other side of the hall" and consequently teachers frequently compare themselves with other teachers. Often they find traits they wish they had in themselves. This makes for uneasiness, shyness, attempts to cover up one's behavior, efforts to create an impression that one is different from the way one really is, and of course this all leads to anger in its many forms.

Feelings not only exist between classroom teachers, but also between classroom teachers and special teachers, such as the art teacher, music teacher, physical education teacher, etc. Mr. Coughlin is the science teacher in a junior high. He naturally feels that science is very important, and our society tends to support the view that sciences takes precedence over other endeavors and interests. He very often has the youngsters in his class work on science projects. These projects are usually complicated, the students become quite involved, and they cannot finish in the three periods per week they have for science. Right after science on Friday, many of his pupils attend music. Several times in the last four months Mr. Coughlin has found himself saying to the pupils, "Well, you can stay on and skip music this week. I'll send a note to your music teacher."

Miss Stein the music teacher, becomes furious when she gets one of these notes. She usually receives them after she has already started her class and after many impatient minutes waiting and wondering why a big chunk of the group is not there. She has specific units in music to get through this semester and a choir that includes many of the children. To her, music is or should be equally as important as science.

Finally she tells Mr. Coughlin off in the teachers' room. He is dumbfounded. His attitude toward music has been that it is relatively unimportant compared to the more "useful" science. He begins to realize his feelings, as a science teacher, toward other teachers. He has been dismissing music as a lower prestige, less important area of learning. He remembers the pupils saying with emphasis, "Do we have to go to music?" He wonders if they were merely reflecting his own feelings of superiority.

Classroom teachers and special subject teachers have other feelings about each other. Sometimes there is jealousy on the part of the classroom teacher because the art or music or physical education teacher can often be more informal with pupils, make less demands on them, put fewer pressures on them, etc. With this kind of feeling, the classroom teacher considers academic subjects more serious, these other subjects more frivolous. If one of the special subject teachers is more popular with pupils, this also feeds feelings of jealousy. Classroom teachers who teach many subjects also resent the extra preparation they must make compared to a special teacher who teaches only one subject.

Special subject teachers have their resentments as well. Mrs. Bay, the art teacher, uses the regular classrooms for teaching art because she has no art room in the elementary schools where she works. The classroom teacher leaves her room during this special period. Mrs. Brock in fifth grade has about the same feelings of possessiveness about her classroom that a cook has about her kitchen. When she returns after art lesson, she always finds something wrong with the condition of the room. Art lessons do make something of a mess, but Mrs. Bay makes a special effort to get the children to clean up, even though it takes a big chunk out of the already meager time available each week to teach art. The fervor of "ownership," the absolute necessity that everything be replaced in its proper place, are important feelings held by Mrs. Brock, and she lets the art teacher know it. Words are spoken, looks are given each time "her" room is used for art.

Needless to say, Mrs. Bay and Mrs. Brock do not have fond feelings for each other, and several times they have exploded with nasty words. Other classroom teachers are less obvious in their feelings, but possessiveness about room "ownership," added to a smug, superior attitude toward art, has made teaching hellish for Mrs. Bay. The children obviously do not do their best in art with a teacher who daily feels this lowered prestige about the subject she teaches.

Special subject teachers sometimes resent being "used" by the classroom teacher. "I don't mind helping with assembly programs," says a music teacher, "but they always wait until the last minute to ask me, as if they think I do no other work in the school." "We have to be at their constant beck and call. They don't realize we teach other classes just as they do," says another. Another special teacher's gripe about the classroom teacher arises from the fact that special teachers have to teach upward of five hundred different children and can hardly get to know each child at all. "They have to know only twenty-eight children. We have to know hundreds. We never know why a child misbehaves, what his special problems are. They have it easy!"

Resentments in school situations develop, as in any work situation, centering on the issue "who gets the hardest job?" Special assignments, after-school supervision, committee work, etc., are usually handled by the principal in an attempt to equalize each teacher's work load. It is, of course, impossible to predict ahead of time how "equal" the assignments will be in terms of time and especially in terms of agony and anxiety. A teacher who is a working mother wants to get home as early as possible because her own children await her. She resents after-school assignments, prefers working through lunch so she can get out early. Often teachers observe her fleeing school right after the last bell, resent her "getting away with things," etc., etc.

Competition inevitably exists as in all situations. Most of it centers on seeking approval from the principal and is discussed in another chapter. Some teachers, however, are just generally more competitive. They like to be on top, ahead of the rest. They want all the special rewards, signs of status, and prestige they can get. To be asked to make a presentation at a PTA meeting on the subject of teaching reading, to go to a special workshop at the request of the principal, to have examples of one's work prominently displayed in the school, to be written up in the local newspaper, are all rewards sought with great fervor by such teachers. Sometimes the needs of the children are lost in this competitive shuffle as the teacher's own needs for prestige in the school or community take precedence over what goes on in the classroom.

One criterion of success that can wreak havoc with teacher morale is how much children achieve in each classroom. Competition based on comparing the achievement scores of each class is even used by some administrators to motivate teachers to try harder. The teacher who even subtly brags about his successes is not well liked by others. The teacher who is successful with a difficult child can easily arouse jealousy feelings in a teacher who has struggled unsuccessfully for many months with the same child.

Another source of strong feelings in a teaching staff is the formation of cliques. Even in a small school, the teachers group together both socially and professionally. There are many reasons why two or three teachers happen to eat and chat together, and why a different two or three form a separate clique. One of them is the experience and age of the teachers. The older, or shall we say veteran, teachers share their commonalities and feelings with each other. It is others like themselves who understand, sympathize, and reassure. The younger, newer, inexperienced teachers also group together to share their common experiences and feelings. They, too, find greater understanding and reassurance among themselves.

Unfortunately, one significant feeling frequently shared by members of one group is hostility toward another group. Some young and some veteran cliques of teachers serve the useful purpose of letting a teacher share her feelings about the other group, "them." Sometimes it appears that sharing common hostilities is the major reason some people join with each other and form a clique. Though this is rarely the sole reason for group formation, hostility-sharing is a highly useful motive. "I just can't stand that young snip" is a feeling that cannot be shared with young snips. The teacher who has this feeling had better be sure she reveals it to someone who feels the same way she does about young snips, otherwise she's in for an argument rather than the reassurance she seeks about the young snip who is bothering her.

New teachers are often disturbed by the confidence, if not smugness, of some veterans. The veterans, in turn, are scared and angry about new teachers, just out of college, who are full of enthusiasm and new-fangled ideas about how to teach. It is often a serious threat to experienced teachers to have a new person with a different approach and attitude toward teaching. Some new teachers act as if everything the veteran has been doing for fifteen years was wrong. This requires the veteran teacher to reject fifteen years of his past professional experiences as inadequate. Few teachers are so weak in self-feeling as to throw away such a big part of themselves.

The new teacher, in turn, must find himself. He must do it himself, in his own way, at his own pace. He cannot adopt the methods of someone else; he cannot be someone else. He cannot merely take over someone else's personal solution to teaching problems. Often new teachers struggle against the suggestions and advice of the experienced person. Obviously, anger, resentment, feelings of inadequacy, and jealousy permeate such a mixture of the new and the old.

How do teachers cope with such feelings, such need for help and reassurance? Sometimes, of course, these feelings fly thick and fast right out in the open. More often they are hidden and disguised. They appear under the surface or in a different form. Mr. Whitehorn, the principal of a large elementary school, feels that teachers should be permitted to express their feelings at faculty meetings. He sets the agenda at such meetings and usually a number of issues, events, and problems are discussed. Sometimes they plan the testing schedule in the school, other times they plan a schoolwide picnic, or even discuss the new reading program, etc. Mr. Whitehorn feels that teachers should express their opinions and views on these issues, and that out of this combined thinking a better solution will be reached for whatever is being planned. Though he expects there will be some disagreement and differing opinions, he feels these can be expressed reasonably and calmly. He realizes that teachers on his faculty have needs for status and prestige, that they feel at times various kinds of jealousies and envies, that they even get angry at each other. It is his view, however, that teachers are (or should be) "mature" enough to "control" their feelings and not let them out socially. The teachers recognize and accept Mr. Whitehorn's point of view about their personal feelings. Therefore, they do not attempt to discuss them openly.

Mr. Whitehorn is pleased with the "maturity" of his faculty. However, when he brings up a typical agenda item, such as the use of the cumulative record cards maintained for each child in the school, something usually happens in the resulting discussion that is out of proportion to the issue itself. Certain members of his faculty express their views with feelings that are strong and vehement. Some appear hurt. Some are clearly angry at each other and at him.

Miss Dockman, an experienced teacher with many years of successful teaching, often takes the position, "Since the way we have been using the cumulative cards works well, why should we change?" Her words carry anger and resentment. Mr. Vines, who is to be rated for tenure this coming spring, appears to be trying like mad to please the principal and remarks, "I believe that Mr. Whitehorn's suggestion is the best." Miss Porcain, a new teacher, wants a number of changes made, and, as she tells her views, her feelings seem to vacillate between feeling angry and feeling hurt and rejected. Miss Post never seems to have an opinion of her own, but tries to placate everyone with,

"That sounds good, too. Why can't we do both?" Mr. Bey, sounding pompous, speaking very slowly and in a low voice, expresses his opinions as if they are full of importance and wisdom: "In my experience working with parents and children over the years, I have found. . . . etc."

The opinions that are being expressed by each teacher are opinions concerning the cumulative record card. The feelings that are being expressed are not related to the cumulative record card at all. They are those very feelings that each teacher has tried, sometimes desperately, to keep hidden inside himself. But out they come, and another agenda item is beclouded, if not drowned with a "hidden agenda" of feelings. As the clock moves on, Mr. Whitehorn usually ends up cutting off discussion before anything is resolved so that he can get on to the next item on *his* agenda. The decision about cumulative records he makes later, alone in his office.

Coping with feelings by attempting to hide them can be an emotionally exhausting experience. Many faculty meetings end in frustration and weariness. Children in the classroom bear some of the brunt of this as the teacher's impatience, irritation, and frustration level are shaken. The day after some explosive faculty meeting teachers spend a great deal of time and energy seeking out each other, sharing their feelings about the meeting, relieving their anxieties and fears. Time spent attending to children is less intense. The teacher's thoughts—and particularly her feelings—are obviously elsewhere.

Teachers also use their colleagues to cope with their own anxieties about achieving "teacherhood."

One of the "by-products" people gain in a working situation is the opportunity to relate to other people. Besides getting a specific job done, many socializing needs are met by contact with other persons during a normal working day. These social contacts have been shown by industrial research to be powerful forces affecting a person's job satisfaction. Teachers can meet some of their own needs for social relationships by their daily contact with children. Children can be friendly, challenging, interesting, and affectionate. However, for most adults, there is an irresistible need to relate to other adults as well.

These social contacts are often brief, but must not be minimized. Adults need contacts with other adults. They need to share their joys and pleasures, their problems and concerns. They need to relate to adults of the same sex and of the opposite sex. Persons who are under the great pressure and responsibility of teaching need the relief that comes from a short chat with another teacher in assembly before the program begins, a greeting in the hall, a comfortable chair in the teachers' room, a cup of coffee, a cigarette, etc.

For teachers, and parents, too, there is a vital need to escape from the total press of child behavior. The noisy, active, insistent, and exciting behavior of children is often very satisfying to teachers and parents. But the need to retreat from the vigor of childhood to a gentle, calming, more "civilized" adult relationship is a special need of adults who are continually in the presence of children.

Often colleagues are of tremendous help to a new teacher or to a teacher who is new in a specific school. In a new job one must leave behind the "ground rules" of the former position and learn the new ones. How strict is the principal about the teacher's "plan book"? Must these records be in by next Wednesday when they are due? How do you get to see the nurse? How do you fill out this form? What do you do about that? Etc.

In some ways teachers gain more help from other teachers than they gain from the supervisor, the principal, the school psychologist, and others whose job it is to assist teachers with a variety of on-the-job problems. It is unavoidable that this be so. It is not necessarily a sign of failure in the supervisor if teachers use other teachers more frequently and more effectively than they use official supervision. The teacher next door is not as available as the supervisor. This availability of other teachers is both physical and psychological. The teacher in the next classroom, the teacher in the teacher's room, etc., are physically available. And when a person needs help, they like it, not later, but now.

The fellow teacher is often more psychologically available as well. Another teacher who is on an equal level understands, sympathizes, appreciates. He is not in an authority position. It is nowhere near as fearful to admit to another teacher that one has problems, whereas revealing too much to the principal can have dire consequences. One can be poorly evaluated, get a bad rating, not be placed on tenure, etc. Revealing oneself to other teachers has dangers too, but they have considerably less potential for bringing about harm to oneself than an authority figure.

Teachers help each other learn how to cope with the principal. How will he react? Will he hold it against me? Can he be trusted? What is he really like? Mrs. Wills is an experienced teacher, but new to this school. It is October and already one child is frequently disobedient. Peter causes her much anguish. It's a particularly rough day today, and she likes to be able to rely on some help with Peter if she needs it. And she feels that today might be a day when she will need help.

Mr. Carter, the principal, has at meetings and elsewhere stated that he is willing to help teachers—"Come in with any of your problems"; "My door is open"; etc. At the last faculty meeting, discipline was discussed. Mrs. Wills was afraid to ask the principal how he felt about teachers sending pupils down to his office when they became serious discipline problems. Mrs. Wills has in the past had a principal who interprets sending a child down to the office as a sign of the teacher's failure. Other principals, however, are quite willing to offer this kind of help to a teacher. Mrs.

Wills didn't want to let Mr. Jones know she was that kind of teacher, not knowing how he would react. She is even unsure how to interpret what a principal means by his words. Mrs. Wills resolves her questions about Mr. Jones in a typical fashion—she asks other teachers what he is like, and quickly discovers what kind of a guy he is. He is really quite willing to have teachers use him for that kind of disciplinary help.

Teachers can also assist each other more directly. Sometimes one teacher has information of value to another teacher. In one school, two brothers from a close family were in two different classes. One brother was very shy, quiet, and withdrawn. The other brother was more communicative, could talk about what was bothering him, etc. When the brothers had special difficulties or were acting up, the teachers of these two boys chatted with each other. The teacher of the more talkative brother could share with her colleague whatever information she had that could help her colleague in dealing with the withdrawn boy. Teachers get help from each other in understanding parents and in dealing with parents. "I had him last year" can be followed with "Do you think it would help if I talked to his mother? What is she like?"

Another direct way a teacher assists is by taking a child out of a colleague's classroom. One pair of teachers used this to great advantage. One of the boys in a fourth grade was slow and often got out of hand. His teacher had a friend down the hall who taught second grade and had a smaller size class. When things got rough, the second grade teacher was delighted to take this boy off the hands of the fourth grade teacher. In second grade this slow fourth grader was a big shot; he knew all the material, felt adequate, and could even help the younger children. His self-esteem was raised by this temporary transfer, sometimes sufficiently so that he could return to his own classroom with enough strength to face the more difficult fourth-grade material. The teachers in this case worked this transfer out on their own, without the knowledge or permission of the principal. Needless to say this kind of help could be arranged by a principal, but in this case these two teachers were able to assist each other on their own.

Teachers on their own learn a great deal from each other by direct transfer of suggestions and ideas. "What worked for me might work for you" is a great source of help and can easily and often does operate outside of the normal channels of supervision.

Perhaps the greatest source of help from colleagues is their willingness to share themselves and their experience; to disclose the personal feelings they have had. Through this, teachers can lose their feelings of isolation and discover a common professional ground.

9

Parents:
Who Is to Blame?

ELOISE IS IN MISS CASWELL'S SECOND GRADE CLASS. FOR A number of months Eloise has been struggling with school and not doing too well. She is a quiet girl, who at times becomes restless and fidgety. She has a great deal of trouble concentrating on Miss Caswell's lessons. She daydreams, shows indifference and apathy. She's not very excited about school or apparently about anything. She rarely responds to Miss Caswell's efforts, and she acts bored and listless. Miss Caswell has tried to get close to Eloise, but with no success. She has even run out of patience, angrily calling Eloise back to the lesson at hand, but even this works only for a few minutes. Miss Caswell has tried everything she can, and nothing works. She has talked to her principal about Eloise and tried several techniques he suggested, but these, too, failed to evoke any response.

In this kind of situation Miss Caswell feels, as would many other teachers, that the problem must be a "home" situation. Since the school has tried many approaches with no resulting change, the source of the problem must lie elsewhere—in the home. Miss Caswell sends a note home to Eloise's mother, Mrs. Becker, and they arrange a conference. This conference is no great surprise to Mrs. Becker. Eloise's report cards have been poor. Mrs. Becker saw Eloise's first grade teacher twice last year because of problems in school.

Mrs. Becker therefore comes to school with apprehension and fear. It's "trouble again at school." Mrs. Becker did not do particularly well as a student herself, although she finished high school. Since being a child, she's been uncomfortable and fearful about school. Eloise's bad experiences merely verify for her what a horrible place schools can be. Miss Caswell tried to put Mrs. Becker at ease with a few chit-chatty comments about Eloise. "Eloise is a nice child," she said. Mrs. Becker translated—"Just as I thought, she doesn't really like Eloise." Miss Caswell made several attempts to raise Mrs. Becker's self-esteem before she got down to the business at hand. The effort was rather futile. Mrs. Becker's self-esteem stayed right where it had been all along, down low.

Now the business at hand. Miss Caswell tried to elicit the parent's cooperation by asking for help in understanding the problem. "Eloise could be doing a lot better in reading, but she seems uninterested in school. Do you have any idea what might be bothering her?"

Mrs. Becker quickly snapped back, "The only thing that's bothering her is school. She's bored stiff." Mrs. Becker interpreted the teacher's question as an attempt to find some reason in Eloise's home situation for her not learning to read.

And Mrs. Becker hit the nail on the head. This, as we have seen, is just what the school was doing—blaming the parents for the child's learning problem. Mrs. Becker, with years of experience coping with school people, blamed right back. The interview was off to a grand start.

The collision of feelings in this interview is not unusual. Both parents and teachers have many feelings that greatly influence their contacts with each other.

Let's take a look at some of the typical feelings parents bring with them when they enter a school building to confer with a teacher about their children.

First of all, there are many feelings that originate in the parents' own childhoods. Parents carry into adulthood many of the feelings about school, teachers, and learning that they themselves developed as children. These residual feelings, ancient though they may be, can powerfully influence a parent's current outlook about school and about teachers. Mr. Abalene only stayed in school until the eighth grade. He did not do very well even when he was in school. He quit to get a job, but also because he was frequently in trouble with teachers. His report cards were usually quite bad, and he did poorly on tests. His feelings about teachers when he quit school were a mixture of awe and anger. Mr. Abalene still feels this way about the teachers who teach his son. After eight years of failure in school, he developed many feelings of inadequacy and failure. As an adult, when he enters the school building, these old feelings emerge. The confidence he has since developed seems to evaporate. He feels and even acts like the small child he once was—a failure, resentful of teachers who put him down, fearful of punishment, and scared.

Many a parent walking past the principal's office in their child's school feels a shudder of fear, a residual feeling from the past, when principals were indeed persons to be feared. Our cultural attitude toward all persons in authority used to be more heavily loaded with fearful respect and awe than it is currently. All authorities—foremen, the police, parents, teachers, principals, etc.—were more frightening persons to children in the past, in the days before authorities were subjected to understanding, child psychology, guilt, and other softening influences. Adults brought up under the more fearful authority often still react to present authorities with some of the old feelings.

It must be mentioned that most of the parents of today did not have happy, successful experiences with school during their own childhood. In fact, until quite recently only 50 percent of the children who started school completed twelve years or graduated from high school. The percentage of dropouts has fallen over the years, but the parents of the children of today attended school when less than 50 percent graduated. The many who did not graduate possess all the feelings associated with being a dropout —regret, disappointment, failure, inadequacy, and resentment.

One must also remember that dropouts often feel jealousy toward the more successful students who succeed and stay on in school. And of course teachers are among that very group of successful people. Teachers were so successful, in fact, they were able to gain admission to college and survive four or more additional years of education. Except in well-to-do suburban school areas, few parents were that successful in school. Most, in fact, dropped out, were behavior problems, were in trouble with school authorities, etc. A significant residual source of parents' feelings is the envy and resentment felt toward the group that made it— in this case teachers. Teachers are, in fact, sadly lacking in one significant experience which would enable them to understand and identify with many children and parents. That significant omission is failure in school.

Interestingly, the dropouts are not the only parents who have residual feelings about their own school days. Those parents who were very successful in school also have strong feelings about school which they bring with them in contacts with teachers. Many a Ph.D. father went through various forms of academic hell for many years in order to obtain his degree.

Many parents when they were students had great anxiety about school success. Dr. Rathbore is an example. He has a Ph.D. in physics from an Ivy League college and is doing research for a large industrial firm. When he attended high school, competition was high. He himself had always done well and was propelled by high academic ambition (translation, pushy parents!) always to do better. If he brought home a report card with only a 98, he was sent back into the fray to return next marking period with a 99, or better a 100. During high school days he diligently and compulsively did his homework. In those days and later in college, if his work was not done, he was unable to get to sleep at night. He never had to face failure, but was literally petrified with fear of the possibility of doing poorly in school. As a parent of a five-year-old in kindergarten it does not appear that this anxiety has lessened one bit. He drives Miss Ferno, the kindergarten teacher, crazy at every PTA meeting. "Are you teaching science yet?" "What about the new math?" "How well is he doing?", etc., etc. His "residual" feelings are hardly residual at all.

Parents have many feelings about their children in addition to residual ones about their own childhood experience with school. Inevitably, the son or daughter is such a personal extension of the parent's self that many a parent feels deeply every hurt, disappointment, and failure that his child experiences. If parents do not fear the child's failure for the child's sake, they may easily, in our status-oriented society, feel their child's failure as a sign of failure in themselves.

A common feeling of parents today is a concern about their own adequacy as a parent. If they have any self-doubts, these are easily aroused by their child having trouble in school. The self-esteem of most parents is automatically raised by their child's school success, and just as uncontrollably lowered by a son or daughter's school failure. Parental egos are inflated and deflated by each report card in direct relationship to the grades on it.

What heightens this concern in our society is the tremendous power of the school in contributing to the child's economic and social mobility. To go up the mobility ladder, you succeed in school. For parents who themselves did not achieve the economic or social aspirations they had for themselves, the child is often handed the mobility baton. "I want my child to go further than I did. I want him to be what I was not." A son nowadays who achieves only as well as his father often feels he has failed. He feels this way because of his father's expectations for him. Parental feelings run high in the lofty arena of school accomplishment, and teachers daily face repercussions of these powerful feelings.

Parents have some other feelings about teachers as well. Sometimes there is a direct competition for a child's interest, affection, obedience. Many a mother is deeply hurt the first time her child speaks lovingly of a teacher. Many a mother feels a sense of failure when the child she has been desperately trying to get to brush his teeth regularly comes home from school one day sold on brushing his teeth. "We had a lesson on personal hygiene and Miss Lemar said we should brush our teeth after every meal." And what really hurts is when the child henceforth actually does brush his teeth regularly.

Some parents, too, give the decisive impression that they are uninterested in school. At all socioeconomic levels there are parents whose primary interests are in areas other than academic learning. They favor athletics, power, fun, or making money over school endeavors. These parents ignore school, rate it as insignificant in their lives, and do not take school failure very seriously. Needless to say this attitude can be upsetting to those who have committed themselves so fully to education.

A significant point should be made here. Many parents from rejected minority groups—Negro, Puerto Rican, Mexican-American, Indian, etc.—reject school, but primarily for defensive reasons. Education has not greatly, if at all, altered their inferior status in the American society. College graduates from these minority groups have been, especially in the past, grossly discriminated against in job hiring and promotion. Schools for these minority groups have often been inferior and segregated. The resulting attitudes of these groups toward education reflect not a lack of interest in school, but instead a lack of hope. Education is not seen as an avenue for social and economic mobility, because in fact it has not been such a vehicle. But these parents have negative feelings about school only on the surface. Their deeper feelings include great respect for education and a deep desire that their children could partake of the real fruits of education.

Another feeling that can affect parents in their relationship with teachers is a real fear of the power of the teacher. Parents sometimes hold back complaints and criticisms or refuse to speak out on school issues. Their primary concern may simply be a fear of retaliation. Parents recognize that all teachers have many opportunities to slight their child, or at least to show less interest, sympathy, and concern for their child. In interviews with teachers, parents frequently find themselves tied up in knots for fear of really telling the teacher what they think or feel. Their concern is that the teacher, consciously or unconsciously, in a normal and natural human way may take out on their child any resentments that they as parents might arouse.

What feelings have teachers about parents? First, and perhaps foremost, teachers most typically make their contacts with parents around some form of trouble. A child is doing poorly, disobeying, or behaving oddly. In many schools this becomes the major reason for teachers to reach out to parents. In some school systems teachers also see parents in conferences or meetings just to get to know them, answer questions, and build a relationship. But even in these schools there are still frequent teacher-parent contacts initiated because a child is having some kind of trouble in a classroom.

The important point here is that if the child is having trouble in the classroom, so is the teacher. As with Miss Caswell in the beginning of this chapter, if a child is not learning or is misbehaving, teachers will try every approach and technique in their teaching repertoire. If none produce the desired change in the child, teachers then typically reach out and utilize every resource available within school. If there is still no change in the child, in one very real sense the teacher and the entire school have failed in dealing with this child. "I'm at the end of my rope. I don't know what else to do" becomes the reason for calling in the parent. The teacher has every right at this point to feel some sense of failure, some feeling of inadequacy.

Some teachers at this point are quite willing (or able!) to admit this feeling and move on from there. Other teachers adjust to this feeling of failure by attributing the responsibility to someone else. This attitude has some validity. "If I have nothing more to offer in changing the child, perhaps someone else can offer a solution." Perhaps Miss Caswell's pupil Eloise herself can do something that will result in her learning to read. Perhaps her parents can do something that will result in Eloise learning to read. Unfortunately, this attitude has within it the feeling of blame. Miss Jones in effect says; "I am not to blame. After all, the other children are learning to read by the methods I use. If Eloise is not learning, the fault lies elsewhere, not in my competence as a teacher." It lies in Eloise herself, in her parents, in the first grade teacher she had last year, even in the principal, who refuses to transfer her to a special, slow class, etc., etc.

Herein, of course, lies the heart of the matter. Most of the difficulty between teachers and parents centers on this very issue of blame. Parents can and do play the same game: "I have done everything I can with Eloise. It's the school's responsibility to teach her, not mine." And parents can become just as skilled as teachers at coping with their own feelings of inadequacy and lowered self-esteem by blaming the teacher, the principal, specialists, or even the board of education.

Bill, in tenth grade, for many years has been doing average work in school. At the same time, his ability testing has consistently revealed that his intellectual ability is above average. This discrepancy between his intellectual potential and his actual academic performance is often labeled underachievement. For years Bill has been so labeled, and frequently his parents have been informed that Bill is "not working up to his capacity." With graduation only two years away, Bill may well have difficulty getting into college. His parents have tried everything in their kit bag of parental techniques, have torn their hair out trying to get Bill to "bear down and get serious" about school.

Bill's teachers, too, have tried every approach available to them. The school counselor has also given special effort, all to no avail.

At the end of tenth grade the guidance counselor again called in his parents. The interview has begun amicably enough, everyone concerned having been made quite aware of Bill's problem. The difficulty was in finding a solution.

The counselor suggested that the parents use stricter discipline at home, more rigid enforcement of homework hours; that they give Bill more chores and responsibilities; that his father spend more time as a "buddy" with Bill, etc. The parents were unable to tolerate this further barrage from the school without in turn offering their suggestions. To each piece of advice offered by the counselor the parents offered in turn a piece of advice to the school—more strict discipline in school, more study-hall time for homework, special classes for pupils with Bill's problem, better teachers (in eighth grade two of his teachers were new and inexperienced, and one eventually quit teaching). Each round of mutual advice-giving and the accompanying blame added heat and then fire to the interview.

One round of mutual blaming went this way:

The counselor suggested gently, "Sometimes it helps if parents insist on regular homework hours and strictly punish the pupil if he doesn't work."

The parents reacted with anger. "Why doesn't the school provide longer, more frequent study halls so pupils can do homework at school?"

This was countered by the counselor with "The lunchroom is used for study hall, and it is not big enough to provide more study-hall time."

Immediately the parents blasted back, "Why don't you build a larger addition to the high school with more space?"

And this was shot down quickly by the counselor with, "The board of education would have to get residents to vote for higher taxes for the addition."

The exasperated, hounded parents (and taxpayers) gave up with, "We are willing to pay the higher school tax. Just ask us!"

In addition to these feelings of inadequacy and failure (whether consciously in the teacher's mind or not), teachers have many other feelings about parents.

Teachers are often emotionally sensitive people and easily aware of feelings in others, particularly children. If a child is having difficulties at home, is emotionally or physically hurt, is not being taken care of properly, etc., the child's teacher may feel deep concern for the child. Often, unfortunately, accompanying this concern for a child is a tremendous quantity of hostility for the parents, who did, or supposedly did, such terrible things to the child. Children who are going through such family crises as divorce can receive much sympathy from a teacher. The parent, in turn, may be the recipient of much anger from that same teacher. The overprotected sixth grader whose mother must personally drive him to school and pick him up after school is missing much in life because of his parent's over-controlling attitude. A teacher can feel sorry for the child but, in addition, would normally feel resentment toward the parent, who is restricting this child so severely. There are extreme cases where children are physically beaten or medical problems not taken care of by parents. In these instances it is almost impossible for teachers to comprehend why parents behave this way. These teachers, therefore, would find it just as impossible to feel sympathy or compassion for these parents, no matter what struggles or private hells of their own these parents might be going through.

Some parents arouse special feelings in teachers because they remind teachers of their own parents. The young teacher who is still struggling against his own parents to achieve independence readily identifies with the child who is also involved in the battle for autonomy. This identification with a child often results in the teacher's seeing the parents of this child in the same light as he sees his own parents. He probably shares with the child the feeling, "My parents don't understand me," with all the accompanying anger, hurt, and regret. Some parents are overly strict. A teacher whose own parents were also very strict in discipline, and who bears anger toward them for being so overly strict, will easily transfer this anger to the overstrict parent of a child in his classroom.

Another example: Miss Brown's father was rather wishy-washy. He was often vague, unsure of himself, and unable to make decisions. For the most part he left the disciplining of Miss Brown and her two brothers to his wife. For many years Miss Brown has resented her own father for what she considers his weak, ineffective role as father. She has a boy in her class, Gordon Sibey. He daydreams, fools around a great deal, and doesn't get down to business. It is Miss Brown's view that Gordon's parents should be more strict with him.

Miss Brown has interviewed Gordon's parents, and, almost as she expected, Mr. Sibey gives the impression of being a lenient, permissive father. He feels that Gordon will "grow out of it," that he, too, "had that kind of problem in school, and yet turned out OK." Mr. Sibey cannot get excited about what is bothering Miss Brown. The very fact that Mr. Sibey is not upset by what upsets her makes Miss Brown even more upset. In fact, she gets furious with Mr. Sibey. Obviously, much of her fury originates in herself. Mr. Sibey's casual, "weak" behavior releases in her all of her own personal feelings of disappointment and dissatisfaction with her own father. She cannot be rational and calm about Mr. Sibey because a father who behaves as he does has very special, very strong personal meanings for her. For this reason, too, she probably can be of little help to Mr. Sibey and Miss Brown has wisely called in the school psychologist who will now be seeing the parents and handling Gordon's problem for her.

Teachers have feelings about parents just because parents are people. Teachers, in a perfectly normal and human way, like some people better than others. Many of the reasons for teachers' liking and disliking parents are similar to the reasons they have for liking and disliking certain children. Parents who possess the kinds of personality traits a teacher favors or feels comfortable with are going to arouse more positive feelings than a parent who has traits the teacher does not enjoy. Some teachers are more comfortable with suave, sophisticated adults, others with calm, relaxed types, others with open, earthy, outspoken persons, still others with intellectual, organized individuals. Any of these factors could affect a teacher's feelings about a parent. Common interests, hobbies, and sports can produce a quick relationship between a teacher and a parent, which might be sadly lacking in another teacher-parent contact.

Other factors that quickly affect a relationship include sexual feelings. Certain women teachers may react with strong envy to any sleekly dressed women who happen to be mothers. A man teacher obviously would have a completely different set of feelings toward such a woman if she were the mother of a child in his classroom. If the parent is the kind of adult a specific teacher normally and naturally avoids socially, feels uncomfortable with, or strongly dislikes, that parent is in for trouble during a parent-teacher conference.

Teachers sometimes feel more comfortable with or try to please a parent from a specific socioeconomic group. Parents of high status within the community, wealthy parents, parents of professional standing, all may receive some special consideration. Sometimes in a fancy suburban school district, the teacher feels inferior, both in status and money, to the parents. This affects their contacts quite differently than in a community where only a few of the parents attended college, and the teacher is looked up to with respect and awe.

Sometimes a very young teacher feels inadequate in talking to a parent of five or six children, trying to "help" the parent understand a fine point of child psychology or child behavior. Teachers who are unmarried occasionally feel uncomfortable about prying into the family life of a child, particularly if it includes discussion of husband-wife problems. But, needless to say, there are some young, unmarried or otherwise inexperienced teachers who are delighted to give advice to parents twice their own age!

As mentioned in other chapters, differences in nationality, race, and of course social class can markedly affect a teacher's feelings about a parent. A variety of feelings can be aroused by such differences: everything ranging from a desire to please to feelings of disgust, annoyance, and anger. Common national, religious, or racial feelings can produce a quick feeling of commonality between a teacher and a parent. Such factors can also produce uneasiness, discomfort, and withdrawal feelings.

Another element in the teacher-parent relationship that can produce varied feelings in the teacher is the authority position of the teacher with reference to evaluating and judging the parent's child. Teachers are in a position where they must almost continually rate a child in terms of success and failure. Grading a child's work, evaluating his answers to questions, and marking tests are a vital part of teaching. They both serve as learning experiences for the child and opportunities for the teacher to judge how well the child is learning. Teachers are then required as part of their responsibility to judge each child's achievement. These judgments are made in regular report cards or reporting interviews, in test scores, and in grading and commenting on work done by the child. Since parents are particularly sensitive to how well their children are faring in the world of school achievement, teachers possess information that is of vital and personal interest to them. "How well is he doing?" "How does he compare to the rest of the class?"

The teacher then is the prime judging authority, the evaluator of the child's performance. The teacher is indeed in a very powerful position. Most teachers are quite aware of the power of this evaluating role in affecting the child's self-feelings, his parent's feelings and ego, the child's reputation, and, of course, his entire academic future. For many parents the grade on a report card plays a major role in determining the child's eventual socioeconomic position and all the comforts and status that implies in our society. Wow! What power the school has! How much the teacher's judgment can influence a child's future!

Many teachers feel naturally some uneasiness and hesitancy about making judgments that might be too hasty, inaccurate, or later prove to be invalid. Often a teacher feels there is potential in a child which is not yet, somehow, being expressed in the child's school work or in tests. Many children are "late bloomers," and some succeed quite well in life even though they did poorly in school. Teachers then have many reasons for feeling uneasy or unsure in discussing a child's performance with parents. Many teachers deal with these feelings by being deliberately vague or by engaging in such double-talk that parents have no idea how their child is really doing.

Teachers do have sincere concern for the child, his reputation, and his future. But they must also deal with their own feelings. Sometimes these feelings are interwoven with very personal feelings about judging others. The teacher may have experienced harsh judgment in his own life and tended, therefore, to shy away from judging others too readily or too severely. He may also have experienced harsh judgment in the past and tended to become just as harsh in dealing with others. "I had to go through it. These kids today should go through it too." The teacher's uneasiness about judging a child can be compounded if a teacher has any self-doubts. The teacher may feel that his own lack of preparation or training, or his own emotional difficulties, contribute to the child's difficulties or poor academic performance. This adds another dimension of uneasiness, if not guilt, to discussing a child's difficulties with parents.

Another area of deep teacher concern in relating to parents is the question in every teacher's mind, "Will the principal back me up in my dealing with these parents?" If the teacher has confidence in an affirmative answer to this question, this will affect markedly his feelings about talking with parents. If the teacher feels that the principal, in order to court the favor of parents, will waver or hesitate to support him, the teacher's position is inevitably a shaky one. If there is a possibility that the principal will clearly support the parents against the teacher, the teacher is indeed in a jam. He feels undercut and undermined. He is out there all alone, on his own. He is bound to feel weak. In a disagreement of this kind with the principal, the principal will inevitably win out. The parents will hear whatever they want to hear from the principal, no matter what position the teacher takes. So the teacher's relationship with his principal plays a large role in affecting his feelings about parents.

Some teachers have special feelings about certain kinds of parents that border on diagnostic stereotyping. Parents of adopted children are frequently misjudged as having a variety of problems as parents. If a child has school difficulties, and it becomes known that he is an adopted child, some teachers automatically stereotype the parents. A diagnosis quickly appears, no matter what the problem, based on the child's adoption. "He's an adopted child" becomes for some teachers an answer to the child's difficulty. This, of course, does nothing to help the parents, particularly since the label is usually uttered by school people with negative emotional undertones.

Children whose parents are teachers themselves may also be in for some stereotyping. Just as some hospital nurses label physicians as the worst of patients, some teachers label teachers in a similar fashion. Teachers who are parents may have special problems maintaining a more perfect or ideal image as a parent. Sometimes they deal with their anxiety over this public image by applying extra academic pressures to their own children. When a teacher is a parent he may, therefore, be in for some emotional labeling by other teachers.

With all these feelings on the part of parents and teachers, the mutual blaming situation described earlier becomes an easy one for teachers and parents to fall into. There are, of course, others as well. One frequent way of dealing with difficult feelings is to avoid contact with the person you feel uncomfortable with. At PTA meetings, for example, teachers often sit together, separate from parents, and are readily spotted in the crowd. Avoiding fearful situations is a normal technique for dealing with fear. It is often difficult to determine which group is more fearful of the other. This discomfort and fear is frequently expressed in discussions where either group has the opportunity to share its feelings about the other.

Developing feelings of superiority over parents is a related method of coping with the variety of feelings that teachers might have about parents. Sometimes this superiority is evidenced by the ease with which some teachers are ready to give advice to parents. At those times when teachers assume an attitude of superiority toward parents, they may also undertake a method of producing change in parents which is doomed to failure. This method is based on the naïve and false assumption that people will change their ways once another person points out to them just what it is they are doing that they should not be doing, followed by advice as to how they should behave. When a teacher decides that a parent's behavior is wrong and should be changed, the teacher clearly possesses smug feelings toward the parent. These feelings easily produce anger and other forms of hostility in parents.

Sometimes teachers are simply just not aware of how naïve their advice-giving is. To tell a parent who is confused, unsure of herself, feeling guilty or otherwise mixed up inside, that she should be firmer and stricter in disciplining a child is pointing out the obvious. The problem for this parent is how to get rid of her confused, guilty feelings. If she were able to rid herself of this inner distress, she would have no trouble being firm.

Another example is the strict parent, who the teacher feels should be less strict. This overstrict parent may be harboring great hostilities, or a special grudge against a child, or she may be harsh for a host of possible reasons. This parent simply cannot turn off her strictness just because a teacher, principal, school psychologist, or anyone else tells her to do so. Parent behavior cannot be controlled the way a valve controls a water faucet. Telling a person to stop being what he is and become something else usually does nothing but create more disturbing feelings.

Teachers often learn to cope with their feelings about parents by a method that in some ways is just the opposite of giving advice. This method requires merely that the teacher listen sympathetically to the parent and permit the parent to get things "off his chest." In this process many parents gain some appreciation and understanding of their own distress. This approach is most effective when teachers admit to a parent their own feelings of distress, frustration, and inadequacy. Often, both parent and teacher can then share their common feelings and work out something together. It is extremely rare for a child to show behavior in school that the parent has not already seen the child exhibit at home. It is just as rare that parents will admit this to a teacher who acts superior to the parent. If the teacher instead copes with his own feelings of distress and failure by admitting them to a parent, at the very least they can commiserate together. Often they go beyond this and work out some common suggestions or agree to get further help somewhere else.

Parents and teachers have a great many feelings in common. The teacher who is also a parent is in an extraordinarily good position to understand and sympathize with the parents of the children in her classroom. Unfortunately, the teacher who is a parent often feels the inadequacies and fear of a teacher rather than being aware of the feelings of parents. Sometimes "teacher-parents" reveal a striking shift in attitude as they discuss the problems their own children might be having with a teacher. They easily view the problem as a parent but then suddenly can shift gears and recognize the point of view of their own child's teacher. This potential ability to recognize both sets of feelings can be a valuable asset.

Since teachers are in the main sincerely interested in the welfare of a child, this can become the focus of contacts with parents. If the teacher is willing to face and admit his own feelings, particularly of frustration and failure, he can usually get cooperation from parents in seeking solutions to the difficulties a child has in school. Most important, by facing and disclosing his own feelings, the teacher can avoid all the defensive blaming that plagues the efforts of teachers and parents to help children learn and grow.

10

Mood and the Teacher

IT WAS ONE OF THOSE DAYS FOR MRS. REILLY. EVERYTHING seemed to go wrong from the time she got up in the morning. She awoke feeling grouchy and irritable. She dragged herself out of bed, made it through breakfast, but hardly. The toast burned, coffee spilled on the clean dress she just ironed. It was a great start for a day and, if anything, things seemed to get worse. Even the car acted up. It usually started easily, but not today. She pumped the gas pedal vigorously, flooded the engine, and took over five minutes just to get out of the driveway. Traffic on the way to school seemed worse than usual, with tie-ups, red lights, and discourteous drivers honking and weaving. She arrived at school in a tense and weary mood. She wanted to turn that car right around and head back home rather than face a full day of teaching. She steeled herself for the inevitable and walked into her classroom in no great shape to face thirty active, excited third graders. Mrs. Reilly felt that if even one child misbehaved today, she would just scream.

Mr. Sheridan awoke today with the sun shining through his bedroom window. He felt rested, relaxed, and good. It was a clear, cool day, and everything seemed just right. He felt great as he ate and drove to work. When he arrived at school, several older boys were climbing on the fence around the teachers' parking lot. He waved to them and smiled. They sheepishly waved back. Mr. Sheridan recalled, ever so vaguely, getting into an argument with one of these same boys earlier this week. Today he just didn't feel like arguing.

Indeed there are those days. The teacher's mood may be just plain rotten and lousy. "Some days you just don't have it." But there are other days, perhaps not too many, when everything seems bright. One's mood is cheery, at peace with the world, an inner calmness, an outer joy. An open, expansive, positive feeling, which includes everyone and everything (well, almost everyone!).

Some of the mood changes are personal, idiosyncratic. Other moods are not so unique but shared by other teachers. Sometimes an entire school is in one mood. The atmosphere pervades the entire building, teachers and children alike.

Sometimes these moods seem to come completely from within. They arise from the depths of our being. They emerge mysteriously and are seemingly unrelated to whatever we are doing with the outside world. At other times our moods are greatly affected by the weather, the day of the week, the time of the month, the period of the school year. Our moods, too, may be greatly influenced by our problems, our struggles, our relationships with the people around us.

The same child behavior that grated one's nerves just yesterday will probably be dealt with mildly or may even be ignored completely in the face of a different mood. The noise, talking, and moving about that is irritating to the teacher at three o'clock was comfortably absorbed by the same teacher at nine o'clock that very morning. Teachers and parents like all human beings are unavoidably inconsistent or varying in both their feelings and their behavior.

The teacher's mood then has a significant influence on the teacher's ability to teach and deal with children. The teacher's patience and irritability, the teacher's sympathy and compassion, the teacher's love and affection, will vary markedly. Sometimes these changes are striking in their contrast, for some teachers' mood shifts are less pronounced, but still evident.

Perhaps the most exciting mood changes are those that seem to be caused solely by some unknown source within ourselves. This is especially gratifying when our spirits rise spontaneously during a time when we are having particular difficulties or crises. The child who appeared hopeless now seems to be responding. The arithmetic material that didn't seem to be getting across now seems to have come through to the children, and they understand it. The child who drives one to tears is behaving nicely. What magic! Has the world really changed for the better, or has our view of it merely been radically altered?

Certainly a consequence of this kind of mood-feeling can be a circular reaction between the teacher and children. On the day that the teacher's mood is positive, the children sense this mood, respond to it, bloom in the glow of it. In turn, the teacher senses this reaction in the children and feels in response that everything in his world is going well. Each positive feeling nurtures a positive response in others, which feed again on one's own positive feeling. Naturally, negative, miserable feelings can also produce a circular pattern. The teacher who wakes up "on the wrong side of her broomstick" one morning easily communicates her depression and tension to children. In turn, many of the children will become more anxious and angry, and some will misbehave and exhibit learning difficulties. This child behavior is destined to add immeasurably to the already miserable feelings of the teacher.

Sometimes it is not easy to separate out from this circular pattern of feeling the specific contribution made by the teacher and that made by the child.

At 3:45 Mrs. Houghton plops into a chair in the teachers' room. Her whole body sags from weariness. Her face is lined with strain, her arms droop over the chair, and she stares blindly at the wall. Thoughts and feelings of the day slowly sort out in her mind. She angrily mutters, "It would have been a great day if it weren't for that Gordon Freedman! He is a troublemaker." As she sits quietly and regains her strength, she recalls how Mr. Snide, the principal, greeted her in the office this morning with a stern warning that her reports were overdue. That kind of bugged her. "He didn't have to be that nasty." Her thoughts wander even further back in time. She didn't sleep too well last night, was up several times, and did not feel rested when she awoke. "It was a rough night." Her feelings quickly returned to anger as she recalls Gordon's behavior that morning. "He was outrageous, defiant. He *is* impossible." Before the anger subsides, she wanders back to her own feelings of weariness of last night. Her recollections and feelings vacillate back and forth between an awareness of her own inner life and a blaming of her feelings on the principal, Gordon, or others around her.

At certain times teachers, like all of us, are more aware of their inner selves, their moods, and the contribution these moods make to the problems of children. At other times the rest of the world seems to cause our problems. Inevitably, teachers sometimes blame others for their own feelings. A child or parent can easily be made the scapegoat for a teacher's inner distress. Often someone else can trigger off a great deal of feeling we are carrying around from last night, last week, or a situation that occurred just ten minutes ago when we felt hurt, rejected, and unimportant.

Moods within each day are influenced by many factors.

The teacher and children's initial mood may set the atmosphere in the classroom for one entire day. Other factors do enter in. Weariness and fatigue play a big part in affecting the classroom mood by the end of the day. Some teachers save special fun activities for the late afternoon, or at least avoid lessons that require great concentration and effort. For some teachers the mornings are just wonderful, but the end of the day brings a "How am I ever going to get home?" feeling. On days when the teacher's schedule has no free periods all day long, that day may begin with a dull, draggy feeling. Teachers inevitably build up pressures throughout the day that need release. The teacher may look forward to his breaks, long for relief. If gym period is canceled or other rest periods omitted, the pressure can become unbearable.

These daily pressures take many forms. One form is self-criticism. "What have I taught today?" "We seem to be going around in circles." "I haven't accomplished anything." Some teachers sense a loss of energy, less ability to try different techniques to hold the interest of children. Sometimes a cup of coffee or a candy bar can restore energy and enthusiasm. Even with breaks and rest periods, by the end of the day many teachers are exhausted. "I feel drained. I'm physically and mentally used up."

Teachers' moods vary with each day of the week. For some teachers Monday is indeed Blue Monday. There is a slowness getting down to work again, an inertia left over from the weekend. It is difficult to shift gears and get back in the saddle. The children may also display the same difficulty getting down to the business of school. Other teachers react differently to Monday. Monday is the beginning of a fresh week, there is enthusiasm and excitement. The children feel eager to learn. For some teachers the relatively unorganized weekend without structure or planned activity arouses anxiety. This tension disappears in the mood of work on Monday and is replaced with planned activity, routine, and regularity.

For some teachers Monday represents a relief from the peculiar malady of our times, "Sunday psychosis." Adults afflicted with this disease feel uneasy, lonely, or anxious with the freedom of Sunday or with being together with other family members. For some teachers the weekend, too, may arouse personal problems and family crises which give way on Monday to the more businesslike, organized, and perhaps more successful world of teaching. This feeling about Monday may make this day the high point of the week, and enthusiasm may slowly simmer down as each day goes by, with Friday being an inevitable low point.

Friday signifies an end or a beginning. An end to the weekly activity, with a kind of longing, if not sadness, for the week just passed and the separation from children and colleagues. For some teachers Friday is a tense day, because it opens up the weekend—cashing one's paycheck, buying the week's groceries, planning for the weekend, looking forward to relaxation, leisure, and friends. On Fridays tempers may be short, and behavior that was accepted earlier in the week is now found intolerable. The teacher may count the hours until school is over. The children may sense or reflect this mood, and they, too, have their own feelings about Friday, which may enhance or conflict with the teacher's feelings about the day.

Some teachers plan fewer involved activities for Friday. It becomes a finishing-up day, a clean-up day, a more leisurely day, in order to mesh with the mood of teachers and children. For some teachers Wednesday is a bad day, for others it is like getting over the hump of the week, followed by easy sledding on Thursday and Friday.

Mood changes during the month are most evidenced by women, particularly as mood reflects their normal menstrual cycle. Premenstrual tension can add considerable feeling to that certain time of the month. The physiological factors that add tension produce varying emotional reactions depending, of course, on each particular woman teacher's mode of reacting and adjustment. Feeling sick or getting over an illness can also affect one's mood, one's weariness, one's capacity to feel energetic, wholesome, and hearty.

Numerous days during the school year influence the mood of teachers and the climate of the school. On the day prior to school vacations and recesses, the mood of the school is usually less serious. It is a day when anticipation is often mixed with the same tensions as on a Friday, magnified many times, depending on the vacation plans and dreams of teachers and children alike. Paydays are happy days. Many teachers celebrate by eating lunch out in a restaurant or, where schedules don't permit this, with other social get-togethers.

Days when schoolwide tests are given, weeks when achievements tests are administered, can also be days of tension and stress. The children inevitably feel concern. Teachers, too, worry about how well their children will do. Final exams are the culmination of much pressure, and they represent the final act of judging with all that it implies for pupils and teachers alike. Other special days unique to a school or to a school system can markedly affect the atmosphere in the entire school; for example, the day before or after a field trip, an assembly period, a school concert or play, etc.

The principal, too, has moods, and these can easily be expressed to teachers in ways that affect everyone in the school. A principal who acts irritable, critical, makes excessive demands, or just looks unhappy can arouse feelings in teachers. "I've got to be on my toes today" adds extra stress to the teachers already overburdened psyche.

Since the school is a part of the community, people in the school reflect the feelings of the world around them.

Events in this world find their way into the school through many avenues. An accident on the street or road outside of school, a fight down the block, the death of someone's parent or spouse or a colleague, may affect the mood of the school.

Television makes instantly available such news events as the war in Vietnam, the assassination of Martin Luther King or Robert Kennedy, the sending up of a space capsule. Reports of such incredible events as these quickly spread through a school, frequently fed by rumors. They add tension, sadness, and anger to the mood of teachers and children alike.

Other days during the school year arouse special feelings. The first day of school is one such day. Many experienced teachers face the first day of a new school year with a mixture of excitement and fear. Some veteran teachers even experience a fright similar to the stage fright of the accomplished actor or actress who still has first-night jitters. Teachers often have difficulty sleeping the night before and exhibit other symptoms of distress before the first day of school.

During the last week of school, teachers and children display many feelings associated with separation and loss. Sadness, crying, nostalgia, and affection are easily expressed. Even children who were perfect horrors will be missed. The teacher may feel loss of a big part of her life as the school year ends, as children leave and move on. The summer becomes a vacuum until the next batch of children appear in the fall. Other times of the year carry special emotions. In snowy climates, the middle of a cold winter becomes "stir crazy" time. Everyone gets on each other's nerves. The opportunity to get away is limited. When the warm, outdoor weather does appear, children and teachers lose interest in school and long for the outdoors and the sun. In other climates, other times of the year carry unique feelings as the weather changes and people's moods follow the changes.

Many teachers deal with their moods privately and secretly. Other teachers reveal them openly to their children and hope for the best. "I tell them I'm in a bad mood, and they respond for a while." Children often do recognize the teacher's mood and respect it. As with other feelings, when they are admitted openly, children are helped to deal with their own varying moods. One teacher reports how a child occasionally comes in in the morning and says "I'm miserable today." "He tells me he would rather sit by himself," she reports. In this way the child helps himself stay out of trouble and learns to deal with his own mood. The teacher's method of handling moods becomes a tool for helping children to learn to live more sensibly with themselves and with others.

11

The Teacher's Private Hell

ALL HUMAN BEINGS HAVE SOME KIND OF PRIVATE HELL OF their own. Some private hells are ever present, long lasting, and more or less permanent parts of ourselves. Other people have hells that arise as crises and are more acute ordeals which slowly fade away until the next personal catastrophe. These private hells are deeply personal. They arise out of our own private worlds, and the emotionally charged worlds we create with family and other people. Different persons wear their private hells in different fashions. Some are more exposed to the outside world and are more obvious to others. For many persons the exposed or revealed portion of their personal torments is like the tip of an iceberg. What is noticeable to most other human beings is only a small and minor portion of the underlying ordeal and misery. Others live fairly continual lives of "quiet desperation."

Many of these purgatories have origins in our past or, at the least, have dim ties to earlier problems. They often reach deep within ourselves and forcibly stir our very being. They may ferment for years, to erupt during some event that is a blow to our self-esteem. They may shake our self-confidence and shatter self-images.

These personal pains have many sources. Unquenchable dissatisfactions with ourselves and unavoidable disappointments are a major source of these more permanent disturbances. Personal and family crises frequently bring these torments to a boil.

The teacher, of course, is not immune to the ravages of these ordeals. Mr. Arlon is a sixth grade teacher. He has been married three years, and his wife is pregnant. She has had one miscarriage. They both very much want to have children and naturally are quite concerned about this pregnancy. On the days his wife visits the doctor, Mr. Arlon's classroom behavior is more jumpy and tense. Though he is teaching thirty children, his mind is preoccupied. He cannot wait easily until his free period. Then he can call her and see how things went with the doctor. He has to use the telephone in the school office. In this semipublic situation he is somewhat embarrassed about speaking to his wife and expressing both his concern and his tenderness. Everyone in the school, of course, knows what he is experiencing at home. Most are sympathetic, some are not. He is a little concerned about the principal's reaction to his obvious preoccupation, his telephone calls, etc.

This situation for Mr. Arlon is relatively temporary, but does affect his feelings in the classroom. Most important, they may arouse other feelings for him as well. Doubts about marriage and parenthood may be aroused as he faces this ordeal. He may have personally disquieting feelings about how others perceive him as he struggles to present an adequate and strong masculine image to the world. He may have fears about how his professional performance is being judged by authority persons and possibly found lacking. Any of these feelings probably trace threads of past agonies to his earlier years, when possibly his masculinity, his competence, and his parent's judgments have had emotionally charged origins.

At any one time in a school faculty a number of these crises, with their accompanying more permanent torments, are being experienced by teachers. A woman whose aging husband has just lost his job and still has three growing children to feed and care for; a teacher-mother who has a chronically ill child or a child with a serious handicap, such as blindness or mental retardation; an unmarried woman teacher who lives with an elderly mother who is chronically and complainingly ill; a young teacher whose fiancé just broke up their engagement to be married and who is still in the shock of hurt and rejection; a teacher going through the agonizing throes of divorce and separation from his children; one suffering the loss of a parent or a best friend; a heart attack striking the father of one teacher; the man teacher who is doing poorly in his job and faces the probable loss of his teaching contract for next year; the teacher whose spouse was killed last year in an automobile accident in which he was the driver; the unmarried woman teacher in her thirties who is struggling to adjust to the strong probability of permanent spinsterhood; the painfully shy teacher who feels left out and rejected; the upset teacher who is fearful that school authorities or colleagues will discover that he is regularly seeing a psychiatrist; the despondent, depressed teacher who secretly and shamefully experiences suicidal feelings; the teacher from a minority group who feels different, discriminated against, highly sensitive to rejection, hurt . . . The list is unending. To be human is to possess a private little hell, a hell of one's own, partially known to few, fully known to none.

How do teachers adjust to such crises and the longer lasting emotional aches in their lives?

The teacher lives, as do all people, many lives at once.

His life in school, vital and time-consuming as it may be, is still only one aspect of the total person the teacher is. At the same time he is a teacher, he is often a child who has parents, he frequently is involved with the opposite sex in some form of courtship, or he is already a spouse in a marriage; he may be a parent with his own children; and he is always a person with friends and a place in a community. All of these lives coexist together. For some teachers, more easily than for others, it is possible to make some separation of these lives, to live each relatively independent of the other. For most teachers, the feelings that are aroused in one area of life spill over or burst out into other areas. The teacher's life outside of school irresistibly arouses feelings that enter the classroom as the teacher himself enters the classroom. And just as forcefully those feelings originating in school are carried by the teacher into his home and his other lives.

Many teachers recognize that their personal struggles and strains are expressed fairly directly in the classroom. Mr. Markus described his first few years of teaching vividly, "I was newly married, filled with values I was questioning, trying to acquire material possessions, and unsure of my place in this society. I had one child, was heavily in debt, and I was moonlighting. I probably worked more hours outside of school than in. I was the worst damn teacher ever to enter a classroom!"

Another teacher describes how when his wife lost a child prematurely after several miscarriages, he elected to stay in school, "But for several days I did absolutely nothing. I was stunned. I sat in the back of the class and had no idea what was going on. The class was carried on by the children. The other members of the faculty were great." One teacher had a visit from a supervisor after a broken engagement, and it was a fiasco.

Other teachers deal with their personal problems in a less direct fashion. Sometimes the changes are subtle, ex-

pressed in a change of one's mood or voice. Other times
there is more obvious strain and less patience. One teacher
whose father died and whose mother was very ill became
very overcontrolling. "I lost my enthusiasm, my spirit. I
kept hold of myself very tightly. I was very calm and controlled. My spontaneity was gone. I couldn't go that extra
mile for the kids."

Still other teachers report a loss of humor, inability to
handle difficult situations, less energy for extra projects,
etc. Most teachers recognize a considerable loss in their
ability to "listen" to children, obviously because they are
"listening" more intensely to their own inner woes.

Some teachers are somewhat more successful. With experience they can make clearer separations between home
and school. "When I come in the door, I leave all my troubles outside." Sometimes the effects are still subtly felt.
One teacher who prides himself on learning to keep his
many personal problems out of the classroom admits that
he has a great deal of difficulty sleeping at night because of
his problems. And when this happens, he is more tired the
next day in school. "So the children lose out anyway."
Some teachers seem able to lose themselves in their work.
In essence, they take the advice to "work hard, keep busy,
and it stays off your mind." Sometimes a teacher retreats so
into work that his behavior becomes almost hyperactive.
One of the difficulties with this adjustment is that sometimes the teacher must stop running, and when he does, all
of his horrors emerge as before. Often the only time a
hyperactive person stops is to sleep at night. Nightmares
and insomnia often plague the teacher who attempts this
type of adjustment.

Teachers who are also mothers sometimes have special
problems of their own. If they leave young children with a
baby-sitter, or get home after their children return from
school, or have to leave in the morning before they get
their own children off to school, they may feel some sense

of guilt about working. A teacher-mother who comes home irritable, tired, and unable to give to her own children may feel a considerable guilt about working. Some teacher-mothers find themselves showering a great deal of interest and affection on one child in their classroom. This may serve as a substitute, if not penance, for not giving enough to their own children

Many teacher-mothers discovered with time that there are values obtained from working (in addition to the money!) that make them better mothers. As they get out in the world, seek professional challenges, relate to other people outside the home, they gain in perspective and personal satisfactions. They become more able to give to their own children than if they stayed home all day, became "stir crazy," and ended up doing a great deal of screaming. Teacher-mothers, too, discover that the amount of time they spend with their own children may not be as significant as the way they actually spend that time.

At times teachers deliberately take a day or more off from work to aid them in recovering from personal problems. Some school districts even permit taking days off for personal "business" without loss of pay. Occasionally a teacher who is struggling valiantly with a personal crisis may drop out of teaching for a year or two. Usually such teachers return to teaching later, and feel they have gained as persons by being able to face their problems honestly enough to recognize their temporary limitations. Sometimes principals will excuse teachers who are in the throes of a crisis from having to participate in extra duties, faculty meetings, etc., as a further aid in fostering recovery.

Many industries are more progressive in this regard than are school systems. Often large industrial concerns recognize that an employee's efficiency and performance are adversely affected during times of personal crisis. These industries meet the problem by hiring counselors, psychologists, and even psychiatrists to help employees during their personal ordeals. These specialized professionals often help employees by fostering self-understanding and by offering human support.

Studies have lent further evidence to this recognition by showing that during personal crises there is a drop in production figures even on the part of the workers on an assembly line. Certainly, employees who have more complicated, creative, and human tasks to perform are often less effective and successful. And what job could be more human, complicated, and creative than teaching! School systems, by recognizing the effects that a teacher's personal crises have on his teaching, might well offer teachers the same opportunity for professional support and self-understanding that industries offer their employees.

Many of us gain considerably as human beings as we struggle through our tragedies. Teachers often feel that their own personal problems enhance their compassion, understanding, and humility. These qualities add immeasurably to the teacher as a human being and to the teacher's success in working with children and with parents.

12

Sex in the Classroom

No MATTER HOW MUCH THE DISCUSSION OF SEX BECOMES publicly and culturally accepted, sexual matters will always remain emotionally charged. Though frank sexual revelation has been changing our sexual values, in no meaningful way does this lessen the highly personal nature of sex and the power of the varying emotions associated with it. Sexuality is not and never will become a rational, mechanistic, unemotional human experience.

Most of the emotionality associated with sexual feelings is due to the many private, unique meanings sex has for each human being. These personal meanings include many additional feelings that considerably enrich sexual experiences and sexual discussions. In different people, sexual feelings are augmented by feelings about their personal adequacy or about their acceptance socially, feelings of fear or feelings of fascination, feelings of intense curiosity or painful shyness, raging anger or bitter jealousies, magnetic attraction or revulsive offensiveness. A host of feelings intermingle with sexual feelings as typical, normal human responses.

The school is not immune from exposure to this entire

177

range of human emotion in both adults and children. Adults of varying experience and children in varying stages of psychosexual development encounter each other within the school, and inevitably many sexual feelings are aroused.

In addition to each individual's unique adjustment to sexuality and all the accompanying feelings and anxieties, age alone adds further complications to the interaction of males and females in the school. In the less recent past there was considerably less public discussion of sex. Older persons in the school, besides coping with normal sexual adjustments of their own age, were brought up in a more inhibited and repressed environment. As a result, some of the older generations of teachers and supervisors may tend to be more restrained, quiet, or inhibited about sexual behavior. Younger children, with the innocence of childhood, are often more open and direct in sexual curiosity and expression. Younger teachers still involved in the freshness of courtship or early marriage, and exposed to more open discussion of sex during their own childhood and adolescence, may also be less fearful and uncomfortable about facing and discussing sexual matters.

Sexuality is expressed in the classroom in many ways by children and teachers—sometimes more openly, other times disguised; sometimes frankly, other times shyly; sometimes comfortably, at other times with anxiety.

The teacher's feeling about ideal male and female sex roles may be especially significant in how the teacher relates to specific children in the classroom. Most adult women teachers identify more readily and strongly with girls, and, correspondingly, men teachers identify more with boys. This identification can take the form of sympathy and understanding for the child of the same sex. It can also take the form of being stricter or even harsher with a child of the same sex.

Mr. Bartolet feels that boys should be strong, independent, and confident. He disapproves of uncertainty or wishy-washy behavior in boys. He interprets such behavior as a sign of weakness, even a lessening of masculinity.

John is a shy, timid soul who has trouble making up his mind. When given a choice of two activities, two books to read, a subject to study, or a project to work on, John takes a long time making up his mind. He vacillates, changes, is very unsure of what he wants or believes.

Mr. Bartolet quickly becomes irritated with Johnny. In his view, Johnny is sissified, more feminine than masculine. Johnny does not fulfill his ideal role of what a masculine boy should be like. The boys in his class who are more confident and sure of themselves obviously receive more spontaneous approval from Mr. Bartolet. His likes and dislikes for boys are greatly influenced by his ideal view of masculinity.

Mr. Bartolet inevitably has views of what ideal feminine behavior is like. This, too, affects his spontaneous likes and dislikes for the girls in his class. He may be especially delighted and pleased by cute, happy, outgoing girls and considerably less interested in shy, withdrawn, unattractive girls. Physical appearance, manners, clothing, and gestures all play a part in defining Mr. Bartolet's ideal sex role. Other men teachers may not share his specific views on ideal sexual behavior. Another man teacher, for example, may value tenderness and sensitivity as outstanding masculine traits and react with pleasure to boys who fulfill this ideal.

Women teachers have their own views on ideal masculine and feminine behavior. These idealized views also differ from woman to woman. Aggressive, active, involved boys may delight some women teachers, while another teacher may be irritated by such behavior. The sex role that girls develop has special meaning for women teachers (and mothers as well). Are the girls interested in sewing, cooking? Are they aggressively interested in boys? Are they more intellectually oriented (or shall we say career-minded)? Do they wear shirts, ruffles, sweaters, mini-skirts, or hippy beads? All this determines whether they fit in or do not fit in to the adult women's view of the ideal feminine sex role.

Obviously, these things arouse feelings about the teacher's own sex role. Is Mr. Bartolet really comfortable and pleased with his own insistence on sureness and independence? Does the quiet, unassuring girl in class make the woman teacher feel less threatened about her own sexuality?

Inevitably children arouse sexual feelings for teachers. At adolescence, these feelings become more obvious, as boys and girls more blatantly discover and display their sexuality. Even with younger children, however, the teacher has some sexual feeling aroused by specific boys and girls. These feelings are no different than the feelings aroused in teachers as they interact with adults of both sexes. They sometimes seem more upsetting to teachers because they are aroused by children.

Many classroom situations where sexuality is aroused take place because of the child's developing interest and curiosity about sexual matters. Some of this sexual behavior is directed toward other children, but a great deal of children's sexual expression is directed at the teacher. To illustrate, young boys may peer under a woman teacher's skirt, stare at her bustline, make attempts to kiss her, hang on to her dress with obvious sexual curiosity. One teacher used the word *caress* to describe the way a boy pupil patted her on the arm. Disgust, repulsion, and anger are not unusual reactions from teachers, particularly older women. There may be pleasure, of course, in the teacher's reaction as well. The young man teacher may be embarrassed as well as pleased by the obvious flirtation or coquetry of young adolescent girls and their sometimes flagrant attempts at dress or makeup. Children from poverty backgrounds, as mentioned in an earlier chapter, may even be more open in their sexual behavior toward teachers. And this arouses even stronger feelings for most teachers.

Young boys in many school settings have crushes on their women teachers. They often express these feelings by wanting to marry their teachers. Some women teachers get frequent proposals of marriage from their male pupils. One teacher reported how "crushed" a boy in her class was because she got married in the middle of the school year. He had obviously been planning to marry her himself! Young adolescent girls, of course, are noted for their crushes, and many a man teacher becomes the object of their romantic interests. This may be expressed by more obviously flirtatious behavior as well as in many less obvious attempts to please, even special efforts to do well academically. Staying after school and hanging around the teacher's desk may also be expressions of hidden and usually vague romantic desires.

Many teachers, men and women, are frankly pleased if not flattered by this special sexual attention from children. This may be especially so if the teacher has any doubts, as many people do, about their own attractiveness to the opposite sex.

Children are often actively curious about the personal life of a teacher in ways which exhibit their sexual curiosity. Direct questioning about the woman teacher's dating experiences—"Do you have any boyfriends?"—are often asked by girls. These girls may be trying to identify and learn from a well-liked teacher what it is to be a female, a woman. Questions about the teacher's marriage and spouse may also be asked. If the teacher reacts with comfortable feelings to these questions, the child can gain considerably in her own sexual development. Teachers may, of course, be embarrassed by such curiosity about what they consider "personal." One attractive woman teacher sensed a great deal of interest in her on the part of a number of boys. She was partly pleased, partly annoyed. "I wish they were as interested in the subject matter I am teaching as they are in me!" Another reaction is to ignore the obvious sexual curiosity about the teacher and fall back on or retreat into subject matter. One male science teacher does this most effectively. The girls in his science class have developed as avid an interest in science topics as they have personally in him!

Some children, too, are very obviously aware of the sexual interest that teachers have in each other. They observe the man teacher seeking out and talking to the pretty teacher down the hall, whether in the lunchroom, the corridor, or other places where it is obvious to children. Gossiping about the rumored romantic interest of one teacher in another is not infrequent. This curiosity is fed considerably if two teachers in the same school become engaged or are married to each other. This event can provide many months of "gossip" for children, as well as for other adults in the school.

Another event that can arouse much sexual curiosity and school discussion is the pregnancy of a teacher. Since many teachers who become pregnant nowadays continue to teach as long as is possible, or permitted, children are exposed to the teacher during most of her pregnancy. They often raise questions, and the teacher herself may share some of her pregnancy feelings and experiences with her class. Pregnancy can provide the opportunity for much child-learning if the teacher's feelings are not too uncomfortable or embarrassing.

Some of the sexual feelings in the classroom are aroused by the active behavior of children who are expressing toward each other their awakening interest in sexual matters. Some children have "boyfriends" and "girlfriends" of the opposite sex at fairly young ages. At younger ages children are open about their curiosity concerning physical differences between males and females. Exploration, touching, doctor and nurse games, etc., are frequent.

In fifth or sixth grade this interest in the opposite sex includes many of the children either directly or indirectly. Flirting, teasing, showing off, and love notes are accompanied by what sometimes appears to be continuous interaction with and attraction toward members of the opposite sex. For some children this preoccupation is great. For all children it has powerful interest and one questions whether sexual interest within schools ever subsides. Teachers at almost all grade levels are confronted with their pupils' interest in the opposite sex. Subject matter in education competes, often unsuccessfully, with the pupils' interest in sexual matters from Junior High on up.

Interest in the same sex on the part of children can also arouse strong feelings for teachers. One very masculine appearing male teacher reported that he "could take the aggressive kids anytime," but he just couldn't stand "effeminate boys." His feelings were strong. "They get to me. I just don't want to be bothered by them." Other teachers react with anger and rejection.

Some children pretend to be members of the opposite sex. "Tomboys" in our culture are generally more acceptable to adults than "sissies." This is probably because the status of males in our society is still considerably higher than the status of females. So boys who exhibit "female" behavior of any kind usually arouse disturbing feelings for teachers. Expressing sexual or body curiosity with others of the same sex, which is "natural" for preadolescent children, can be upsetting to some teachers who see homosexuality as an inevitable result. The two boys who go into the cloakroom together to explore secretly some obvious sexual matter may be especially upsetting.

Another form of sexual behavior evidenced by young children in the classroom is masturbation. Children, whether out of curiosity or to relieve tension, may handle their genitals or press their legs together in obvious sexual rhythm while in the classroom. Teachers react with varying feelings to child masturbation. Most teachers "intellectually accept" such behavior as normal, inevitable, and unharmful. Emotionally, however, masturbation can readily produce a different set of reactions in a teacher. If not embarrassment, certainly feelings about the social unacceptability of masturbation are readily felt by teachers. Some teachers are appalled by a child displaying such behavior in public. Feelings can run high about this mode of sexual expression.

Educational events in the classroom may have sexual connotations or cause sexual arousal. A picture portrayed in a film in geography class showing a Polynesian mother breast-feeding her baby, cutouts of magazine advertisements displaying ladies undergarments, poetry and literature with direct or indirect sexual references, observations of animals openly having bowel movements, or animals displaying their genitals during the class trip to the zoo, the study of animal and human bodies in biology class—are all examples of learning situations that arouse sexual feelings for children. The teacher then is often confronted with giggling, whispering, etc.

Where sex education is directly a part of the curriculum, the teacher is forcibly faced with sexual reactions and questions. Some teachers deal with the children's tremendous curiosity in sex education class by sticking rigidly to biological and physical explanations and discussions. Other teachers attempt more open discussions and deal with petting, the pill, and the host of other normal areas of sexual interest.

Menstruation seems to receive more attention than other developmental sexual experiences of children. This is undoubtedly because in our consumer-oriented society, menstruation has great commercial interest. The companies that sell products for girls to buy have for many years produced booklets and films on menstruation with the obvious intention of selling their products along with educating the young girl. Since the advent of boys into adolescence is not accompanied by a similar commercial need, there has been less interest in educational material for boys. Because of this lack of public interest, male adolescent behavior may be more embarrassing for teachers to cope with.

Adjustments made by teachers to their own feelings and to children's feelings about sexual matters vary considerably. Some teachers react to the crude, awkward, and often unsuccessful attempts of children to emulate adult sexuality with a great deal of sympathy and understanding. One woman teacher recalls vividly the crushes she had as a child, particularly when she was in sixth grade. She now teaches sixth grade and is able to react tenderly and sensitively to the sexual expression of her pupils. Other reactions are more severe. Some teachers get angry and attempt to directly forbid such behavior. "We don't do that kind of thing in school." Other teachers discuss issues such as dress and manners openly with children. Still other teachers, whether as part of the curriculum or not, discuss the sexual questions of children in the classroom. Many teachers, and parents too, have discovered that the first few times they discuss sexual issues with children, they are most uncomfortable. After many discussions, adults more freely toss around terms like *penis* and *vagina* and communicate to children more normal and comfortable acceptance of sexuality.

There are, however, still powerful forces in ourselves working toward discomfort about sex. There is no reason why teachers should not have the same range of hang-ups about sex as everyone else in our society. In addition, our sexual values are changing, and teachers, like everyone else, may be confused or unsure about what they really believe. Such sexual issues as the pill, virginity, the double standard, premarital intercourse, etc., are issues that concern teachers personally. They also concern the older children they teach. These are the very issues about which our entire society has differing viewpoints and varying feelings.

Perhaps in this area of life, more than in almost any other, the teacher learns as he teaches. He may find himself forced to question his own sexual beliefs as he faces the probing, open sexual interest of children. He may gain comfort and ease in sexual discussion by the experience of discussing sex with children in the classroom or in private conferences. He can better understand his own humanity as he faces the human yearnings and questions of the child who seeks a real education.

13

Race in the Classroom

MRS. FERRARI TEACHES SECOND GRADE IN AN INNER-CITY
school. She is white. More than three-quarters of the
pupils in her class are black. Mrs. Ferrari was brought up
in an Italian neighborhood. There were few Negro pupils
where she attended school, and she had no Negro friends.
Even in college there were only a handful of Negro students, and they tended to congregate by themselves.

Until recently Mrs. Ferrari's contacts with Negroes have
been minimal. She views herself as open-minded and un-
prejudiced in her feelings about race. She herself chose to
teach in a predominantly Negro school, even over the objection of her parents. Compared to her parents and their
generation, she considers herself quite liberal. She likes her
teaching and has fond feelings for many of the children in
her class. She has met most of their parents, and, though
she feels a little uneasy with some of them, she sees them
mainly as conscientious, sincere people who are deeply
concerned about their children. Few of them fit into any of
the stereotypes she has heard about Negroes.

She does, however, have one obvious problem in which

race plays a part. This problem is with Charles. Charles is an active, mischievous black boy, who gets into trouble so frequently that Mrs. Ferrari feels the need to discipline him. But when she gets to the point of pressuring Charles about his behavior, he reacts in a way that disturbs Mrs. Ferrari no end. He looks her right in the eye and blurts out, "You're only picking on me cuz I'm colored!" This reaction shakes her up, leaving her sometimes in utter confusion. Why does this bother her so? She knows full well she is not picking on Charles because of his race. Or is she?

Mrs. Ferrari and many teachers like her feel uneasy, uncomfortable, about Negroes. Considering the degree and intensity of conflict between the races in this country, these feelings are certainly neither rare nor peculiar. Nevertheless, it bothers her to feel this way. It occasionally results in her avoiding her responsibility to discipline Charles. She finds herself backing away from potential conflict with him and letting him get away with things she would not let other children do.

Feelings about race in this country are disquieting to say the least. They can quickly bubble over into a variety of negative and guilty feelings, explosions of hate and acts of violence. These feelings are well known between the white and black races, but feelings also run high between whites and Puerto Ricans, whites and Mexican-Americans, whites and American Indians.

The important feelings that are aroused by racial differences in the classroom are primarily feelings of superiority and inferiority. The white majority group in our society has maintained a superior position of power, status, and wealth for many years. Inevitably accompanying this position are feelings of superiority, righteousness, and prestige. In general, the white majority possesses these feelings toward all minority groups. These superior feelings are the heart of all majority-minority group problems whether between two racial groups, two religious groups, two socio-economic groups, two occupational groups, etc.

Though superior-inferior feelings are important themselves, they create additional feelings for many majority group members. Most human beings feel some sense of wrongness or guilt when they are in a position of advantage over someone else, or when they are well-to-do and others are poor, or when they are accepted and others are rejected. Many whites feel some sense of guilt about the superior feelings and actions of their own majority group.

Some whites, of course, immediately cover up their guilt with a host of defensive measures, including hostility, prejudiced remarks, etc. These defensive remarks always portray minority group members as lazy, worthless, passive, trouble-making, immoral, sponging, etc. These defensive devices serve only one purpose—to convince whites that minority groups are truly inferior and therefore to relieve any guilt about feeling or acting in an arrogant way.

For many years whites were able to cover up this guilt by avoiding situations where the inferior position of nonwhite groups was evident. This avoidance was accomplished by segregation, ghettos, and discrimination. In recent years, however, nonwhite groups have made many successful and dramatic efforts to face whites with their true feelings. Militancy, demonstrations, marches, even riots have served as acts of recognition. For many whites, they have increased the general awareness of the inequitable relationship between the races.

Whites in the classroom, child and teacher alike must therefore cope with these feelings of guilt and hostility toward Negroes or other minority groups. It is probable, for example, that Mrs. Ferrari had problems disciplining Charles because her uneasiness was compounded by feelings of guilt.

If the majority group's feelings stem from a superior position, the minority group has consequently to cope with an inferior position. Unavoidably, the minority group—with its minimal power, status, and wealth—feels inferior, downtrodden, hurt, and rejected. These feelings may well be expressed in the classroom. Such feelings are also easily turned into anger.

Racial feelings can become especially awkward when, as is usually the case, a class is composed of mixed races. Fighting is liable to occur along racial lines, and for this reason some teachers prefer a segregated class, because this does tend to cut down some of the racial tension among the children. If the teacher is of a different race than most of the children, this, too, produces more opportunity for racial feelings to be expressed.

Hostility is a normal feeling for children to feel and express in the classroom. But racial anger adds a new and more dramatic dimension to normal hostility. There are many opportunities for fighting to include a racial element, or for racial feelings to be aroused as children naturally have blows with each other. The teacher has to cope with her feelings about this kind of fighting and, in addition, her own feelings about race. Hostility may be directed toward the teacher either because she is a teacher, or because of her race, or both. Angry children may use such terms as "white bitch" or terms like "cracker" when they feel anger at a white teacher.

When the Reverend Martin Luther King, Jr., was killed by a white man, tremendous hostility toward whites was expressed by Negro children in the classroom. One white teacher reports that when the children realized that King was killed by a white man, it was as if for the first time they became vividly aware of the fact that their teacher was also white. She felt most uneasy and had a strange, alienated feeling about children whom she knew well and loved. Racial conflict in the local community or elsewhere in the nation inevitably arouses such feelings for children and teachers alike.

Since any discipline can arouse hostility in children, the white teacher may be the recipient of ordinary anger over discipline which is compounded with racial hate. "I don't have to mind you, white teacher!" "I'm not gonna mind you white people."

Negro teachers also have to cope with racial anger from Negro children. Mrs. Hall is a Negro. She teaches a second grade composed mostly of Negro children. Arthur is a playful, energetic black boy who sometimes gets out of hand. He snatched a pencil from one of the white boys in the class and teased him about it. Mrs. Hall stepped in and told Arthur he had to return the pencil. Arthur quickly blurted out to the other children, "She's just taken up with those white kids." Mrs. Hall finally had to explain to Arthur that she could not permit anyone in the class to take things from anyone else. She emphasized that if the occasion occurred, she would protect Arthur the same as any other child in the class. Arthur never accused her of favoring whites again. But to be accused of being an "Uncle Tom" in the classroom gave this Negro teacher a few rough moments of inner turmoil.

When prejudice is expressed by younger white children, they are usually repeating what they have heard from the adults around them. One teacher in a mixed class overheard a white child say to her Negro friend, "My mother said that Negroes are dirty." The term *nigger* may be used by children in anger or otherwise. Typical stereotypes about Negroes are also repeated. Mrs. Smith, a first grade teacher who happens to be Negro, heard a white girl in her class say in anger to her Negro friend while they were arguing, "Negroes are mean, they like to fight, curse, and kill each other." Mrs. Smith calmly dealt with this situation by explaining that "you can find that kind of behavior in all races." Several children pointed out that Mrs. Smith was black and didn't act that way at all. The two girls quickly restored their friendship, but Mrs. Smith and other Negro teachers are frequently confronted with racial feelings in the classroom. One white first grader innocently told her Negro teacher, "My mother said I had a *nigger* for a teacher," and then spontaneously added, "I think you're beautiful."

Teachers as a professional group undoubtedly reflect the full range of racial feeling and prejudice that exist in our entire society. It is unavoidable then that within the school teachers will express racial feelings and prejudices to each other. Often these feelings are expressed unconsciously—the prejudiced teacher is not fully aware, if at all, of the impact that a remark, a phrase, or a comment may make.

Typical remarks in the teachers' room and elsewhere carry racial feelings in a disguised fashion. These remarks might even appear to the white teachers who utter them as devoid of racial feeling. Critical remarks made about persons on welfare or the unemployed are sometimes made with no obvious racial feeling, but are readily interpreted by minority teachers as reflecting some innate prejudice. Tales told about how Negroes or other minority races nowadays are receiving preferential treatment in hiring are a frequent source of such feeling. Remarks like "You've got to treat them harshly—it's the only language they understand" reflect a racist view about all Negroes. Emphasis on such statistics as "thirty percent of the Negro families in this school have no father in the home" seems to ignore what must be an equally valid fact—that the other 70 percent of the Negro families in this school *do* have a father in their home.

Many white teachers who have deliberately chosen to teach in all-white schools have definite racial feelings when Negroes or other minority group members are transferred to their school in order to achieve some integration in the classroom. Open enrollment, busing plans, bringing together the children of different races for special curriculum projects and programs—all this often arouses racial feelings in teachers who have deliberately chosen to avoid contact with minority groups.

Teachers are also exposed to racial feelings in the community at large. One white teacher reported the reactions of onlookers as she took her predominantly Negro kindergarten class for a walk in the community around the school. Most of the persons living near the school knew some of the children or were their parents. Their responses were friendly and favorable. They waved at the group of children walking two by two and were pleased with the school and the teacher. A few short blocks away, the neighborhood changed, becoming predominantly white. Bystanders ignored the children. The teacher entered a grocery store to buy the children cookies and was shocked when the man behind the counter actually refused to sell her cookies for "those children."

Teachers get it from other sides as well. Young white teachers who choose to teach in the inner city often have to cope with negative reactions from their own parents. If they are in conflict with their parents, their choice of school feeds the fires of parent-child battling. Socially, teachers have to face remarks like, "You poor thing, you teach in an inner-city school?" One education professor, evaluating a student, said, "You are too intelligent to waste your talent working in the slums." The barrage of negative racial feeling hitting the teacher can be tremendous.

In addition to various hostile feelings, teachers often face feelings of hurt, rejection, and fear which are aroused by the poor relationships of the races in our society. Young children who have not as yet learned to cover up their hurt usually express these feelings more openly. Often white teachers who have not previously faced the full impact of racism in our society are amazed at the depth of feeling in minority group children.

Miss Hedrick teaches first grade. She is white, a warm,

affectionate person, and particularly sensitive to the feelings of children. Perhaps partly because of this, the children in her class easily reveal to her what they feel. Most of them are Puerto Rican or Negro. One day the class went on a field trip to a candy manufacturing concern in the downtown area. The streets were crowded with white faces. Several of the children were clearly afraid and not just of the crowds. They hung onto their teacher and her assistant: "Will they like me?" "Will they hurt us?" seemed to be their fear. An older, twelve-year-old white girl was especially friendly to them. They were surprised, almost startled. Back at school several children announced with obvious pleasure, "She's my friend." This same class had earlier discussed with great concern the assassinations of Reverend King and Robert Kennedy with the feeling that "white people are killers."

Another white teacher reported young children talking about race with great fear and then suddenly asking, "Do you still love us, Mrs. Ferno?" "Why wouldn't I?" she answered. "Because we're colored," one child responded.

Teachers naturally respond to these expressions of feelings with many feelings of their own. Minority group teachers have to make the same adjustments to prejudice that all minority group members make. Bitterness mixed with determination or loss of faith in the white bureaucracy that controls the schools is not an unusual reaction. Many teachers maintain a great deal of affection and kindness in their relations with children of all races. But the inner strain, the emotional turmoil, may be great and is not easily hidden.

On the other hand, feelings of understanding, love, and compassion which develop between members of different races can be equally powerful. They develop between teachers out of friendship and shared experience. They develop between teachers and children out of the learning relationship itself. One white teacher put it this way, "It makes me feel humble. I am the first white person these kids will get to know well. This will make a lifelong impression on them. The responsibility is enormous."

14

Dealing with Feelings:
The Encounter with Self

THROUGHOUT THIS BOOK, CHAPTER BY CHAPTER, THE EVI-
dence has grown: The teacher does inevitably experience,
in the classroom, the full range of human feeling. The
young, inexperienced teacher described in the introduction
to this book, was overwhelmed by her feelings. Many
teachers feel this kind of reaction in themselves at some
time in their educational career. Other teachers are more
frequently troubled by their feelings, often quite acutely.
Every teacher and parent in daily contact with children
has his times of concern and trouble, his times of disturbing and upsetting feeling.

When the teacher does become aware of his inner
life—his feelings—there are inevitable questions. "How
can I deal with these feelings?" "What are some of the
answers and solutions to these kinds of situations?" "How
do I get out of this mess?" "What is the best way to cope
with myself?"

These questions can take on a pleading, demanding

tone. "So what do I do about it?" "Give us some answers." "Tell me what to do!" "How would *you* deal with this kind of situation?" These questions can even become angry in tone. Resentment is expressed. "You never give us answers"; "You never really solve anything"; "Talking doesn't help."

Learning to deal with one's feelings is a profoundly personal process. There is no easy technique or method that can be copied from others. There is no simple process of seeking solutions or answers from others which may then be imitated by the troubled teacher as a means of dealing with his own feelings.

Sometimes "taking" a technique or method from another person does seem an easy way out. "What should I do?" is the question asked, and the answer given (by another teacher, the principal, or some educational specialist) is, "Why don't you try this?" or, "When that happened to me, I did . . ."

Occasionally, but rarely, such direct imitation of a method "works." By works, one merely means that the immediate problem or feeling disappears or is reduced to more manageable proportions. More frequently, however, taking over someone else's solution just doesn't work for many reasons. The heart of the matter is that each person must find his own solution to coping with himself and living with his feelings. This solution must be individually attained, because the ultimate technique or solution is nowhere near as significant as *the actual process we engage in to achieve our unique solution.*

Mrs. Smith is having trouble with a stealing problem in her class. Johnny has occasionally been involved in taking pencils from other children, and once was accused of "stealing" a book. These situations quickly settled down and did not seem serious. Yesterday, however, as she entered the classroom Mrs. Smith caught Johnny fumbling around in her purse on the desk. He was embarrassed about being caught, and she was unsure how to deal with him. She postponed the confrontation with him by telling him she would talk to him about it after school at the end of the day.

During the day she had the occasion to chat briefly with several more experienced teachers in the lounge. Since Johnny's problem was on her mind, she mentioned it to them. They were quick to sympathize and to offer their own experience.

Mrs. Franklin said, "You've got to be strict with those boys. They need to know right from wrong. I punish them right away."

Mrs. Argo offered, "I call in the parents and tell them what happened. They usually get after the child, and it never happens again."

Mrs. Ferridale reacted differently. "I just ignore it. It will probably stop. Most kids do some of this and grow out of it."

Miss Putney, the school psychologist offered, "He's probably seeking attention from you. We had a situation like that last month. The teacher assigned the child to be her helper. She praised him a great deal, and the kid's doing fine now."

Mrs. Smith had listened carefully and patiently. But as she left the teachers' lounge she was confused, to put it mildly. Whose advice should she take? Even in seeking professional advice from physicians or technical advice from automobile or TV repairmen, you can generally get as many different opinions as the number of experts you seek out. In such a situation you can even solve your problem neatly by finding the expert who will support you in the solution you have already decided upon for yourself.

The problem with human behavior, of course, is that there is *never* just one reason why a child behaves in a certain way. There are always many antecedent factors, all of which eventually affect how a child behaves. Johnny may steal because it will get him attention from the teacher. He doesn't get attention from the teacher because Mrs. Smith dislikes his whining, clinging behavior. He whines and clings because at home he has discovered that whining, clinging behavior is the only way to get attention from his mother. His mother otherwise ignores him because she is having a marital problem. One of the reasons she is having a marital problem is that her husband is having problems with his job where his adequacy and masculinity are threatened by his boss, etc., etc.

Mrs. Smith wants to know why Johnny steals. Because his father is being treated badly by his boss? Because she (Mrs. Smith) dislikes clinging behavior, which is due to the fact that as a child her mother punished her because she herself clung or was too dependent? Why did the teacher's mother react to clinging this way? What about her mother? Who started all this? Adam and Eve, of course. Where else can Mrs. Smith go with this kind of thinking?

In addition to this problem of attributing responsibility, children may behave in a similar way but for a completely different set of reasons. Mrs. Franklin offered her explanation for stealing: "Be strict. I punish them right away." Mrs. Franklin may be right. If a child steals because of lack of firmness at home, strictness might be called for. However, she may be dead wrong. If he steals to get the teacher's attention, firmness will probably do nothing to solve his problem and may, in fact, make him feel more rejected by the teacher. Moreover, he may steal for other reasons; for example, to get money to buy the friendship of his peers. Obviously, if this were so, it would certainly be preferable to help him get along better with other children. Firmness will not even begin to help him with his inability to make friends, if that is what really troubles him.

What with all these factors affecting the child's behavior, you would think finding a successful solution was knotty enough. What further complicates this entanglement is the feelings the teacher has about stealing and about the child. The teacher who believes in sternness often wants to stamp out stealing because it angers her. Mrs. Franklin may have been treated harshly as a child when she did wrong, and her tone is consequently punitive and unsympathetic.

Miss Fernale feels more sympathy for the child. Another teacher may even feel sorry for him. Still another teacher feels deeply hurt that a child will steal from her purse. Another teacher may feel a deep sense of failure as a teacher because a child in his class behaved in such a fashion. Mrs. Smith's personal feelings about stealing may be still different.

Since the teacher has such feelings, the advice she attempts to follow may be doomed to failure because her own feelings are completely inconsistent with the technique being suggested. The teacher who feels sorry for children, or who feels hurt, cannot feel stern and strict at the same time. The teacher who feels anger cannot react with sympathy. Many a parent gets tied up in knots trying to follow an expert's advice when his own feelings are just the opposite of those required by the advice. When child "experts" believed in scheduled feeding of infants, many a warm, flexible mother simply could not feed her child on a schedule rigidly set by the clock. When the experts changed their advice and began recommending unscheduled feeding whenever the child was hungry, well-organized mothers revolted against such flexibility. The result in either case was confused feeding experiences and probably mixed-up babies. So Mrs. Smith has to explore her own reaction to stealing in order to discover her real feelings about Johnny's behavior.

Still another factor militates against advice-giving. The teacher who merely copies the advice of another does not exercise her own intelligence or understanding. She learns to deal with stealing by being strict, whether it is called for or not. She does not apply her own compassion and empathy, her own experience. She does not understand why she is using the method she is, only that it sometimes works. She cannot understand why it does not work in those situations where it is not relevant.

Copying other people's advice does nothing to develop the inner resources and strengths of the teacher. The teacher gains no understanding of the child, and, more important, she gains no understanding of her own feelings and reactions. It is an approach that denies the teacher's own self—her competence, understanding, and ability. It denies her the abilities she needs next week or next month, when faced with another case of stealing, which probably will have different causes and possibly arouse different feelings. Advice-giving reduces the teacher's independent competence in coping with future problems. It usually renders the teacher more dependent on such others as the principal, school psychologist, other teachers, the books, etc.

And if you are still unconvinced of the limitations inherent in advice-giving, consider the reality of the teacher's own behavior in the classroom. For the most part the teacher reacts automatically to child behavior. The teacher acts on her own feeling, not on the basis of what someone told her to do. She reacts spontaneously on the basis of her own being at the moment. She rarely has or can take time to count to ten, then carefully consider the advice of others before she acts. We behave for the most part, painful though it may seem, *without thinking*. The behavior we express is a part of ourselves. If we are to react differently next time, we ourselves must be different next time in some way. We can spontaneously and automatically deal with a child in a new way only to the extent that we ourselves have become new.

How do teachers change themselves so they may spontaneously feel or behave differently next week or next month?

The process seems to be one that arises out of the very

being of the teacher. With courage, with humility, with a certain sureness, the teacher says to himself, "This is it, fella, get down to business," or, "I said, kid, you'd better do something," or, "I finally stood on my two feet and said the hell with the theory course." Sometimes this inner strength is conscious; the teacher is aware of it. The teacher actually faces himself as a person, talks to himself, pulls himself up "by his bootstraps." Other times the process is unconscious. There is less awareness of it, less conscious understanding of what is going on while it is going on. Sometimes the process appears to the teacher only as he looks back. Then and only then does some of it seem to make sense, to fit together, to become a piece.

This encounter with oneself is a purely personal experience. No one else can do it for the teacher. It is the ultimate in loneliness, as described by Moustakas in his book by that title.

Each teacher must make her own way, deal with her own self. And yet, other people can help or hinder this process. Others can support the teacher's struggle, ignore it, partake of it, or share it.

Whether informally or spontaneously, others can help. More formally planned conferences or discussions can also help if properly handled. In either case, the real essence of external help is the sharing by others of their own true selves, their own feelings, their own real life struggles. To the extent that others—whether they be teachers, parents, or children; supervisors, principals, or professors—offer of themselves personally, that is the extent to which the teacher is supported in her own struggle for selfhood.

These sharing experiences can take place in the teachers' lounge, brief meetings in the hall, in talks after school, during drinks at the local bar, or any informal setting where meaningful human contacts are possible. These self-encounters can also take place, although they do so less frequently, at meetings, seminars, courses, and workshops.

Certain requirements in the external situation seem to enable the inquiring teacher to engage more effectively in self-encounter.

It is imperative that the interaction between the teacher and others be based on sharing of actual personal experiences. If involvement of the participants does not begin by discussion of personal experiences, it must do so eventually in order to be personally meaningful. Sometimes discussions begin elsewhere; perhaps with a case study of a child, or exploration of such a topic as social development, or a problem a child is having in the classroom, or a discussion of some theoretical or research issue.

Self-encounter becomes possible as participants add to this initiating topic a sharing of their own feelings and experiences. Not just Johnny's case study, but what did I (the teacher) do, how did I feel, what were my thoughts and experiences? Obviously it seems easier to ensure this kind of "happening" if it is defined as such from the beginning. Rather than choose such a topic as social development of children, let's call the topic "fighting," which is usually the real issue for teachers or parents. Discussing fighting can very quickly bring forth accounts of personal encounters—yesterday in the classroom; my own fighting as a child with peers; my two children at home who fight and tease each other; my arguing with the principal. How do I deal with my own disagreement with others? Should I use physical punishment? How do I feel about hitting a child? When is hitting acceptable to me: ever, in riots, in Vietnam? Should police use force? Have I ever been hit by someone? How did I feel? How did I react?

The inquiry is endless, the exploration is personal, the discovery is enlightening. The process may be disquieting, painful. The more personal and real it becomes, the more the process becomes agonizing. Teachers discover that within themselves is a mass of contradiction and confusion. There are no clear pathways, no guides, no basic principles, no answers; only a process, an encounter with oneself which can have personally gratifying results.

A crucial requirement for this kind of sharing is some reassurance to the teacher that such discussion will not cause him to feel hurt. He has real concern that his reputation might be damaged, his ego deflated, that others will look down upon him, value him less as a human being. Sometimes when the inner pressures are so great, teachers will spill out their feelings without concern for any such external consequences. At these times the teacher can no longer hold in what must be expressed.

Frequently after such a spilling-out experience, the teacher feels guilty about revealing so much of himself. What reduces this fear of being hurt is the reaction of others. If they, too, share their innermost selves, it is reassuring to reveal himself. If there is an authority person present (the principal, a parent perhaps, the school psychologist, etc.), that person's reaction is especially important. Does he disapprove? Is he shocked? Or does he, too, engage in self-disclosure and become personally involved? A principal relating his own experiences in the classroom without any ego-heightening embellishments reveals his humanity to teachers and encourages them to safely reveal themselves.

One of the responses that typically kills this kind of sharing is the person who quickly offers an answer, a solution, a technique that will solve the particular problem being discussed. Why bother exploring one's feelings about fighting, disagreement, hitting a child, and the like, if all you have to do is "keep the child after school for one week, and put him to work washing blackboards?" If such a solution is actually accepted by the inquiring teacher, all thinking, all exploration, all understanding will stop. Sometimes authority figures feel that the prestige of their position requires that they have answers to all problems of teachers. If they seek this prestige by offering answers to the problems teachers reveal, the experience of self-encounter never gets off the ground. The principal makes his point. Teachers may either agree or disagree with the authority, but sharing of personal experience becomes extremely precarious, if not impossible. In this case, if one uses one's personal experience, it can only be to verify or disagree with the answer of the principal. Personal experience is then not a means of self-discovery but is used as a weapon in the battle against or in support of the authority. Needless to say the principal may not be the only person who seeks prestige through giving answers. Other teachers can also cut off discussions by this method.

The most meaningful value gained by these discussions is the surprising discovery of commonality. Most human beings put tremendous effort into covering up their real being, disguising their true selves, hiding their feelings. The result is that teachers and principals may find themselves interacting with each other as if they were phantoms or shadows, their real substance not revealed, but hidden, invisible.

In self-revealing discussions the feelings of others are discovered, and the excitement of this discovery can be a joyful one. "I feel that way, too." "It lets me see inside others." "I found that others had lots of problems." "That drives me crazy, too." "I know how you feel." The discovery is tremendously reassuring to one's feelings about one's own normality. "I thought I was going crazy." "I feel normal, like everyone else." "The feelings I had about myself as a person and a teacher are not so different." Briefly, too, it can open a window through the depths of human loneliness. "I learned or confirmed that others share my worst guilt-producing experiences." "I thought I was alone." "I'm not the only one who has problems." "There are others who also have a feeling of inadequacy."

There is relief in the discovery that one's secret, private feelings are not really so different, so abnormal. There is heightened self-regard as one discovers that teachers who were putting on such exteriors as success or calm or sophistication were feeling underneath their own private fears, inadequacies, hurts, and angers.

The encounter with self is not merely a self-revealing but a self-discovery process. The teacher discovers how he feels about children's behavior, and about himself. He discovers some of his values as a human being and becomes aware of contradictions and confusions within himself. "I understand myself better." "I have a much better appreciation of the whys of my behavior." "I have looked at myself and some of the things I saw I did not like, and still I am very grateful." "My negative feelings regarding one of my own children are very clear to me now." "I can look at myself more clearly." "I have become aware of the shades and depths of my emotions." These are all typical teacher reactions to this kind of process.

That the process can be painful, there should be no doubt. As we look within, embarrassing contradictions appear. "I want children to be obedient, but to be independent, too." "I don't believe in physical punishment, but when I get furious, I hit a child." "Sometimes I believe in violence, sometimes I don't." "I want to like Jane, but I just don't."

Facing the real limited existence of oneself as a human being produces heights of misery, loneliness, hopelessness, and fright. "I feel I cannot solve everything," but "I'm still unhappy with this. I still always want to do what is "correct." "I have anger against myself because of my inability to cope with outside problems." "I have a feeling of disgust with myself for not stating things I wanted to." "I feel I have raised my ideals in teaching so that I will be even more comfortable about such things as punishment and anger." "My shortcomings seem much more pronounced to me now." "As I take that inward look, my comfort in some situations will be lessened." "This is a good way to solve problems, but evidently painful."

So the process of self-encounter is accompanied by both positive and negative reactions—feelings of hope and of hopelessness, of expansiveness and limitation, of joy and misery, of excitement and depression.

There are no easy, pleasant, and comfortable ways to live meaningfully with the fullness of human emotion. There are, of course, other methods which further help teachers to deal with their feelings. These methods assist the teacher particularly in coping with feelings when they are extreme. These are the typical, normal techniques all persons use to spill out, fend off, or otherwise deal with feelings on more of an emergency basis. Many teachers take home feelings that are aroused in school. At home they may be shared with a sympathetic roommate, a spouse, or a friend. Also, they may be displaced on persons at home. Getting angry at a roommate, a spouse, or one's children is a typical displacement method.

It is typical of most human beings that they let their hair down within the confines of their own family, as they would never do in public. Teachers who are charming, delightful creatures at school can easily turn into glowering monsters at home. Here they are able to release their real feelings in the comparative comfort and safety of the family. Children and parents normally use the family for this purpose, as an escape valve and a place to be themselves.

One teacher reported that her husband could tell what kind of day she had at school by the supper she served. If it was a well-cooked and lovingly prepared meal, her feelings were great. If it was a TV dinner, watch out! Some teachers, as mentioned earlier, keep busy—clean, or occupy themselves with other work that may serve to keep their mind off disturbing feelings temporarily. Some teachers find religious experience deeply rewarding. Meditation and solitude can be most useful, particularly for self-analysis. Recovery from disturbing experiences often takes place during vacations or retreats, or just when seeing different people and new places. One nun reported that she and her sister teachers had difficulty recovering from the problems of the teaching day because the entire school staff lived together in the same convent. They needed the opportunity to meet other people, nonteachers and persons from outside their school situation. Recovery can sometimes be fostered by changing schools, changing principals, even changing hairdos, etc.

There are, of course, many patch-up, temporary techniques. The Scotch tape or bailing wire approaches to holding oneself together work better for some teachers than for others. Denying, blaming others, feeling sorry for oneself, and covering up can sometimes be effective, at least for a while. Daydreaming, tranquilizers, and alcohol may offer temporary respite.

Some teachers utilize psychotherapy for help in coping with and understanding their feelings. Jersild (see Bibliography) has reported extensively on the value of counseling, psychoanalysis, and other psychotherapies for teachers.

Feelings aroused in school can be released in activities far from the school building. One teacher drives ten trafficless miles each day and finds release in his car. Other teachers have sports, hobbies, and such activities as dramatics, which permit steam to be released. Becoming involved, if not engulfed, in professional activities can provide status to a low-feeling teacher and may at the same time add to one's profession. Even watching television, besides being relaxing, can serve to let off steam. The typical example is that of the little old lady watching the TV boxing bout from her rocking chair and screaming "encouraging" words, "kill, kill, sock it to em!" For some teachers anger can be released even this way.

There are then many ways for teachers to deal with their

feelings. One way or another, sooner or later, the teacher engages in some kind of encounter with himself. This encounter thrusts the teacher directly into the joys and the torments of his struggle as a human being.

The teacher is perhaps more fortunate than most human beings today. Few persons today engage in deeply personal encounters in their chosen vocation. The teacher has a rare opportunity to develop his own humanity each day in his work.

15

Uniqueness:
The Paradox of Self-Discovery

WE HAVE SEEN THAT TEACHERS GAIN A GREAT DEAL AS they discover the similarities they share with other teachers. The teacher is gratified to discover that others have experienced the very same feelings as he. This sharing is a significant ingredient in the process of discovering the meaning of one's humanity.

Reassuring as this awareness may be, the teacher gains even a greater reassurance in self-encounter. He recognizes and accepts in himself that which is unique to himself. *No other me is identical to me,* nor was there ever an identical me, nor will there ever be. No other me even slightly resembles me in the complexity of my person, in the richness of my past life, and in the very special way in which I interpret the world.

Each teacher, then, is different from all other teachers, from all teachers living now, and all teachers who have ever lived or will ever live. Each teacher is a very special human being, a unique person. Each and every person who is called a teacher is unlike all others who are also called teachers.

This uniqueness is inevitable, it is unavoidable, moreover it is inviolate. This uniqueness cannot be eradicated to produce identical teachers, similarity of teaching, or uniformity of classroom teaching behavior. In spite of efforts that might be made to achieve uniformity of teaching performance, the uniqueness of each teacher irresistibly emerges and manifests itself in the classroom. No matter what energies might be directed by supervisors toward maintaining a uniform standard of teaching performance, each teacher highlights his own special talents, abilities, and strengths. This uniqueness effectively negates the concept of a minimum uniform standard of teaching to which all approved and successful teachers supposedly conform.

The teacher cannot adhere to an external standard. He must express his own self, his own idiosyncratic pattern of interests, experience, and excitement. This pattern is identifiable solely as his own, just as his fingerprints are solely his own. This book is replete with examples of the variation and distinctiveness of teachers—one teacher loves music, another science; one is delighted by order and organization, another enjoys confusion and clutter: one teacher can be firm and strict, another nurturing and warm, etc. Each teacher, as we have seen, has his own likes and dislikes, his special feelings for specific child behavior. Chapter by chapter the feelings of teachers described in this book methodically destroy the myth of teacher uniformity and similarity.

If the teacher attempts to be what he is not, either to please himself or to gain the approval of others, he expresses a façade in the classroom. This façade is shattered, sometimes rarely, oftentimes frequently, by the teacher's inability to deny to children what he truly is. Directly or indirectly his real self will be revealed. Maintaining this disguise places a teacher under the considerable strain of a most agonizing human conflict—the denial of self.

The fact of a teacher's uniqueness has many implications. Each teacher possesses his own special collection of traits or characteristics. It is impossible for any one teacher to possess all traits, all characteristics. No single teacher can be equally competent in all the qualities of being a person. One cannot be equally delighted with music, with science, with painting, with geography; one person cannot respond with equal emotion to both dependent boys and independent boys; one person cannot be both cautious and impulsive, strict and nurturing; one person cannot relate equally well to six-year-olds, nine-year-olds, and fourteen-year-olds. One cannot be everything. One can only be what one is—a limited human being. No teacher or parent can be perfect in everything, in all ways, in all qualities.

This is the reality of human limitation. Any specific trait or characteristic a person has of itself limits his ability to have other traits or characteristics. You cannot possess an enduring characteristic and also possess it opposite. If you are a cautious and careful person, you cannot also be impulsive or spontaneous. There are times when caution is called for in dealing with children. At other times spontaneity or impulsiveness might be more appropriate. Any one teacher or parent cannot meet both situations with the same adequacy. If you express emotions easily and openly, you are not a person who is emotionally reserved or distant. At times reserve and calmness are helpful in working with children. At other times or with other children the opposite trait might be more appropriate. Any one teacher or parent cannot offer both kinds of behavior with the same sincerity and adequacy. If a teacher is fervently excited about nature and especially animals, this fervor will be communicated to children. They will sense this special excitement, respond to it with interest and learning. If the teacher's "thing" is nature and animals, he cannot possess the same fervor for numbers, literature, mathematical symbols, painting, and innumerable other educational interests. Every teacher is limited. All human beings are.

Mr. Jones is considered a strict teacher. He is fair, just, good with children, and when it called for, he can be stern and strict. He believes deeply in obedience and order. These are outstanding traits in his personality. The principal, for example, sends to Mr. Jones's class those boys who seem to need strict treatment, and Mr. Jones usually succeeds with them. To be stern and strict requires that Mr. Jones not feel too deeply the hurts and disappointments of children. He does feel ready sympathy for the need of children to be controlled by adults. Mr. Jones is not cruel nor is he cold or harsh with children. He is, however, unable to feel great concern for the troubles of children—their hurts, their sorrows, their rejections. Mr. Jones's particular strength, his strictness, does not require that he be sensitive to other needs in children. He is sympathetic to their needs to be limited by adults, to the lessened anxiety some children feel when they sense that a teacher means it, no matter what. This trait is outstanding in Mr. Jones. But because he possesses it, he cannot feel sympathy for the hurt, pain, and disappointment children can feel. Every human strength or attribute carries within it a built-in limitation—the inability to possess an opposing attribute.

Is Mr. Jones a good teacher? Of course! Does he understand children? Yes, but some children more readily and sympathetically than others. He has the normal limitation of all human beings. If both he and his supervisors recognize this, he can easily be a superior teacher. The children who need what he has to offer can be funneled to him. For those children in his class whom he does not understand well, he can rely on other teachers to help him.

Often Mr. Jones talks with Mrs. Peck down the hall about the children he does not seem to understand. Mrs.

Peck has a different set of strengths. She feels hurt, sorrow, rejection easily. She senses them readily in others. Her strengths balance out Mr. Jones's strengths. She, too, inevitably has her own limitations caused by her strengths. She has difficulty being stern with children; her strength, her sensitivity to their hurt, gets in the way. Mr. Jones sometimes helps her out by dealing sternly with a child in the hall or by backing up her discipline.

Neither Mr. Jones nor Mrs. Peck possess all the ideal characteristics theoretically called for in a teacher. No one teacher can. Mrs. Peck will never, no matter how hard she tries, become like Mr. Jones. Mrs. Peck may attend a course offered by a top-notch college professor, visit a psychoanalyst regularly, or in some other way make a determined effort to learn, to change. She will probably learn much and change much, but she will never acquire the uniqueness of Mr. Jones, nor lose her own uniqueness, her strengths, and her limitations. What she may gain, hopefully, is an increased acceptance of her own limitations. This acceptance could help her to lean more heavily, without resentment or envy, on persons like Mr. Jones, who has those very abilities she herself does not possess.

The next implication of the teacher's uniqueness is highly significant. Teachers typically look at most of their own traits and characteristics judgmentally. Some traits are viewed as positive, good, admirable; others are perceived as less good or bad, as negative or as weaknesses. The teacher then sees himself (and others, too, may look at him in this way) as possessing some traits that are strengths and others that are weaknesses.

A crucial point here is that the negative judgments we apply to ourselves are purely arbitrary, relative, and inappropriate. These negative judgments are moreover often self-destructive. *The same trait that is viewed as a weakness can also be viewed as a strength.* Each and every limitation can be perceived as a positive, needed, and therefore useful, attribute. We have seen how every strength in the teacher automatically limits him as a person; it is just as valid that each limitation has within it a potential strength. Mr. Jones was limited in his ability to recognize and sympathize with the hurts of children. But this very limitation permitted him to be strict. If he did not have this limitation, he could not comfortably and readily apply strictness in his dealings with children. His "weakness" can be viewed from the completely opposite point of view. The same trait is no longer a weakness but rather a strength.

Sometimes merely the choice of word that we use to describe a trait carries within it the emotional judgment of strength or weakness. Is stubbornness a strength or a weakness? If instead of choosing the word *stubborn,* we substitute the term *persistent,* we now clearly have a trait most people would perceive as positive. The same characteristic can be perceived any way we like. Whether we call it *stubbornness* or *persistence,* this trait can be a limitation or a strength. Sometimes it is appropriate, at other times flexibility, compromise, or some other trait is necessary.

Whether the teacher perceives his traits as strengths or weaknesses has important implications for the teacher's ability to accept himself. Since he cannot possess all traits, or be perfect in every way, he inevitably has limitations. These limitations, if viewed as weaknesses, often make it difficult for the teacher to accept what he truly is and to give the best of himself to children. Typically, instead of experiencing his "limitation" as a strength, the teacher views it as a weakness. He then tries to eliminate the trait from himself. Since many of these characteristics are basic elements in the teacher's self, they cannot be eliminated. At best they can be partly hidden, disguised. The teacher who instead views his limitations as potential strengths, builds on these attributes and gives more fully of himself to children.

Miss Barnes is an example. She considers herself a shy person. As a child she often shied away from other children and was uncomfortable in the presence of strangers. Though she became more outgoing, underneath she is still a truly shy person. For many years Miss Barnes judged her shyness as a weakness. She felt deeply all kinds of real and imagined losses in her life, which she attributed to her shyness. During her first few years of teaching she felt her shyness prevented her from relating to children in an outgoing, vivacious manner, as she observed several other teachers in her school apparently doing. There was never any doubt in her mind that her shyness limited her competence as a teacher and was in fact a serious weakness in her teaching.

With experience and some effort at self-encounter, Miss Barnes began to look at herself, the same self, differently. Her shy, quiet, unobtrusive manner encouraged certain children to express themselves, accept help from her, and come out of their shells. Her gentle, tender manner of relating was completely appropriate for these children. Interestingly enough, these same children were terrified and extremely uncomfortable in the presence of the vivacious, outgoing teacher down the hall. Miss Barnes has discovered that her shyness is indeed a strength, a useful, needed attribute in her work as a teacher. She can bring out and foster the development of certain children in a way no other teacher in the school can. Her uniqueness is a value in her teaching. These children are now gaining a great deal from Miss Barnes. Prior to her self-encounter, Miss Barnes used to reject these children. They reminded her too painfully of her own "weakness." She wanted to stamp out in them the very trait she was trying to stamp out in herself. There is no longer any such need. It is not a weakness. The very same trait is now a strength, a great value in her teaching.

Teachers then become specialists. Each teacher has a very special, very unique "thing" to give to children. When he gives his uniqueness to children, he gives the very best of himself. If he tries to give other things to children, as he must, he may be successful. He is, however, nowhere near as effective as when he is giving what he has most to give.

As children move through their school careers, they are, fortunately, exposed to a tremendous variety of teachers. Hopefully, each child somewhere along the way will find one or more teachers who give to him fully that which he most needs, that which will most help him in his own life struggles.

The uniqueness of the teacher is truly the essence of his humanity. His special way of relating, his own specific feelings, his own talents and abilities, his own excitement as a person—these are what make teaching the highly rewarding task it can be. By offering his true self, the teacher exercises the greatest influence on a child's development. This truly is teaching at its best.

Bibliography

Brown, Claude, *Manchild in the Promised Land*. New York: Macmillan Company, 1965.

Holt, John, *How Children Fail*. New York: Pitman Publishing Corporation, 1964.

Jersild, Arthur T., *When Teachers Face Themselves*. New York: Bureau of Publications, Teachers College, Columbia University, 1955.

Jersild, Arthur T., and Lazar, Eve, *The Meaning Of Psychotherapy in the Teacher's Life and Work*. New York: Bureau of Publications, Teachers College, Columbia University, 1962.

Jourard, Sidney M., *The Transparent Self*. Princeton, N.J.: D. Van Nostrand Company, Inc., 1964.

Morris, Van Cleve, *Existentialism in Education*. New York: Harper and Row, Publishers, 1966.

Moustakas, Clark E., *Loneliness*. Englewood Cliffs, N.J.: Prentice-Hall, Inc., 1961.

Sartre, Jean-Paul, *No Exit*. New York, Knopf, 1947.